# Coastal Circulation and Sediment Dynamics in War-in-the-Pacific National Historical Park, Guam

Measurements of Waves, Currents, Temperature, Salinity, and Turbidity: July 2007–January 2008

By Curt D. Storlazzi, M. Katherine Presto, and Joshua B. Logan

Open-File Report 2009-1195

U.S. Department of the Interior
U.S. Geological Survey

**U.S. Department of the Interior**
Ken Salazar, Secretary

**U.S. Geological Survey**
Suzette M. Kimball, Acting Director


U.S. Geological Survey, Reston, Virginia 2009

For product and ordering information:
World Wide Web: http://www.usgs.gov/pubprod
Telephone: 1-888-ASK-USGS


For more information on the USGS—the Federal source for science about the Earth,
its natural and living resources, natural hazards, and the environment:
World Wide Web: http://www.usgs.gov
Telephone: 1-888-ASK-USGS

Suggested citation:
Storlazzi, C.D., Presto, M.K., and Logan, J.B., 2009. "Coastal Circulation and Sediment Dynamics
in War-in-the-Pacific National Historical Park, Guam. Measurements of Waves, Currents,
Temperature, Salinity, and Turbidity: June 2007–January 2008." USGS Open-File Report 2009-
1195, 79 p.

# Contents

# Figures.

# Tables

# Appendixes

# Coastal Circulation and Sediment Dynamics in War-in-the-Pacific National Historical Park, Guam

**Measurements of Waves, Currents, Temperature, Salinity, and Turbidity:**

**June 2007–January 2008**

By Curt D. Storlazzi, M. Katherine Presto, and Joshua B. Logan

## Introduction

Flow in and around coral reefs affects a number of physical, chemical and biologic processes that influence the health and sustainability of coral reef ecosystems. These range from the residence time of sediment and contaminants to nutrient uptake and larval retention and dispersal. As currents approach a coast they diverge to flow around reef structures, causing high horizontal and vertical shear. This can result in either the rapid advection of material in localized jets, or the retention of material in eddies that form in the lee of bathymetric features. The high complexity and diversity both within and between reefs, in conjunction with past technical restrictions, has limited our understanding of the nature of flow and the resulting flux of physical, chemical, and biologic material in these fragile ecosystems.

Sediment, nutrients, and other pollutants from a variety of land-based activities adversely impact many coral reef ecosystems in the U.S. and around the world. These pollutants are transported in surface water runoff, groundwater seepage, and atmospheric fallout into coastal waters, and there is compelling evidence that the sources have increased globally as a result of human-induced changes to watersheds. In Guam, and elsewhere on U.S. high islands in the Pacific and Caribbean, significant changes in the drainage basins due to agriculture, feral grazing, fires, and urbanization have in turn altered the character and volume of land-based pollution released to coral reefs. Terrigenous sediment run-off (and the associated nutrients and contaminants often absorbed to it) and deposition on coral reefs are recognized to potentially have significant impact on coral health by blocking light and inhibiting photosynthesis, directly smothering and abrading coral, and triggering increases in macro algae. Studies that combine information on watershed, surface water- and groundwater-flow, transport and fate of sediment and other pollutants in the reef environment, and their impact on reef health and ecology are essential for effective reef management.

Two of the main anthropogenic activities along west-central Guam's coastline that may impact the region's coral reef ecosystems include pollution and coastal land use/development, as discussed in the review by Porter and others (2005). The pollution threats include point-sources, such as municipal wastewater (Northern District, Hagatna, Naval Station Guam, and Agat-Santa Rita Waster Water Treatment Plants), cooling water (Tanguisson Steam and Cabras Power Plants), and numerous storm water, ballast water, and tank bottom draw outfalls; nonpoint sources include septic systems, urban runoff, illegal dumping, and groundwater discharges. Poor land-use practices include development without the use of runoff management measures, increased areal extent of impervious surfaces and decreased extent of vegetative barriers, and recreational off-road vehicle use. Furthermore, feral ungulates and illegal wildfires remove protective vegetative cover and generally result in increased soil erosion. While anthropogenic point-sources have been reduced in many areas due to better management practices, nonpoint sources have either stayed constant or increased. Between 1975 and 1999, it is estimated that Guam lost more than a quarter of its tree cover, and more than 750 wildfires each year have resulted in a greater proportion of badlands and other erosion-prone land surfaces with high erosion rates (Forestry and Soil Resources Division, 1999).

Approximately 1.8 square kilometers ($km^2$) of Asan Bay, west-central Guam, lies within the National Park Service's (NPS) War-in-the-Pacific National Historical Park's (WAPA) Asan Unit; the bay is the sink for material coming out of the Asan watershed. Anthropogenic modifications of the watersheds adjacent to Asan Bay, which include intentionally-set wildfires, construction, and agriculture (Minton, 2005), are believed to have increased over the past 25 years (National Resource Conservation Service, 1996). These land-use practices cause accelerated erosion by removing grasses and small trees that stabilize the soil. While even modest rains on Guam cause sediment plumes to be discharged from many rivers to coastal waters, including the Asan River (Minton and others, 2007), typhoons pass close enough to Guam every 2-3 years to cause heavy precipitation (>2 cm/hour) on the island, rapidly flushing unstabilized soil down to the coast and onto WAPA's nearshore reefs (Porter and others, 2005).

Observations by Minton and others (2007) suggest that this terrestrial sediment discharge to the coastal waters has resulted in sedimentation, eutrophication, and pollution that has impacted WAPA's coral reef ecosystem. These authors have shown that sediment collection rates in tube traps on the fore reef of Asan Bay's fringing reef are very high and the trapped material is predominantly composed of fine-grained terrestrial sediment that typically has nutrients, bacteria, and pesticides adsorbed to the particles; the trap collection rates are both spatially and temporally heterogeneous. Work by Minton and others (2007) further shows that the input of terrestrial sediment to the park's nearshore waters is greater during the wet season (July-December), which is of serious concern as this is also the time of peak coral spawning and larval settlement (Richmond and Hunter, 1990). Observations by Minton (2005) and Minton and others (2007), however, suggest that while large quantities of terrestrial sediment are being collected in traps on the fore reef and often covered their coral recruitment tiles, the reefs themselves are not being buried by mud, suggesting that oceanographic processes are sufficient to limit net sedimentation on the fore reef. Quantitative information on the deposition, residence time and advection of this fine-grained terrestrial material through the bay's fringing reef system, along with the controls on these processes, is needed to better manage the WAPA's marine resources.

Because of these observations, the Asan watershed is an area of concern to the NPS and was designated as one of the U.S. Coral Reef Task Force (USCRTF) Guam Local Action Strategy's (LAS) priority watersheds. In 2007 the U.S. Geological Survey (USGS) Western Coastal and Marine Geology (WCMG) Team initiated an investigation of coastal circulation, sediment flux, and sediment residence time along west-central Guam, primarily focusing on WAPA's Asan Unit.

This work also supports the USCRTF's goal of investigating the impact of land-based pollution on corals reefs. Furthermore, the data collected during this experiment will provide NPS and the Guam Environmental Protection Agency (EPA) with quantitative baseline data for possible future measurements made during the planned large-scale expansion of the U.S. military installation at Apra Harbor, which is less than 2 km south of the park, and extension of the Hagatna Water treatment outfall, which is less than 4 km north of WAPA's Asan Unit.

## Project Objectives

In 2007, USGS and NPS researchers began a collaborative study to determine coastal circulation patterns and sediment flux along west-central Guam, and in particular, in WAPA's Asan Unit and its coral reef ecosystem. To meet these objectives, flow and water column properties along west-central Guam, and in WAPA's Asan Unit in particular, were investigated using a suite of meteorologic, fluvial, and oceanographic instrument packages. The continuous measurements of winds, rainfall, river discharge, waves, currents, tides, and water properties (turbidity, temperature, salinity, and light) from these instrument deployments provide information on nearshore circulation and the variability in these hydrodynamic properties for WAPA's Asan Unit. These data will complement ongoing and future water quality efforts along west-central Guam and in WAPA and will provide baseline information of the hydrodynamic and oceanographic regime for the marine portion of WAPA's Asan Unit.

The field experiment consisted of continuous collection of oceanographic, meteorologic and sediment data in WAPA from July 2007 through January 2008. In October 2007, the USGS and NPS recovered, downloaded, cleaned, repowered and redeployed the instruments. The goals of the experiment were to understand the episodic delivery of sediment to the bay and its residence time in the bay. In order to do this, the USGS and NPS set out to do the following:

a) Measure wave heights, wave periods, wave directions, current speeds, current directions, temperature, salinity and turbidity to provide baseline information to NPS and others.

b) Measure wind speed, wind direction, rainfall and barometric pressure to: (1) provide baseline information to NPS and others; (2) address forcing of oceanographic data, and (3) provide boundary conditions and calibration information for a 3-dimensional, hydrodynamic numerical model for west-central Guam's waters.

c) Determine flow and transport (sediment, contaminants, nutrients, larvae) patterns for different sets of forcing conditions.

d) Acquire digital time series imagery of the study area from a land-based camera system to document surface conditions and plume dispersal pattern(s).

e) Determine the influence of oceanographic and meteorologic forcing on plume and seafloor sediment dynamics.

## Study Area

This study was conducted along the west-central coast of the island of Guam, Mariana Islands, USA (fig. 1). Guam lies between 13.2°N and 13.7°N and between 144.6°E and 145.0°E, and has an area of 541km$^2$. It is the southernmost island in the Mariana Islands and is the largest and most heavily populated island in Micronesia (Office of Insular Affairs, 2008). The northern part of the island is a forested coralline limestone plateau rising more than 260 m above sea level while the south is primarily highly erodible volcanic terrain with peaks as much as 406 m that are covered in forest and grassland. A coral reef surrounds most of the island, except where rivers discharge into bays. The island's population is most dense in the northern and central regions. Guam is described by the Pacific Islands Global Climate Observing System (2008) as having a tropical marine climate, with an average annual rainfall of 2,260 mm, ranging from 2,000 mm to

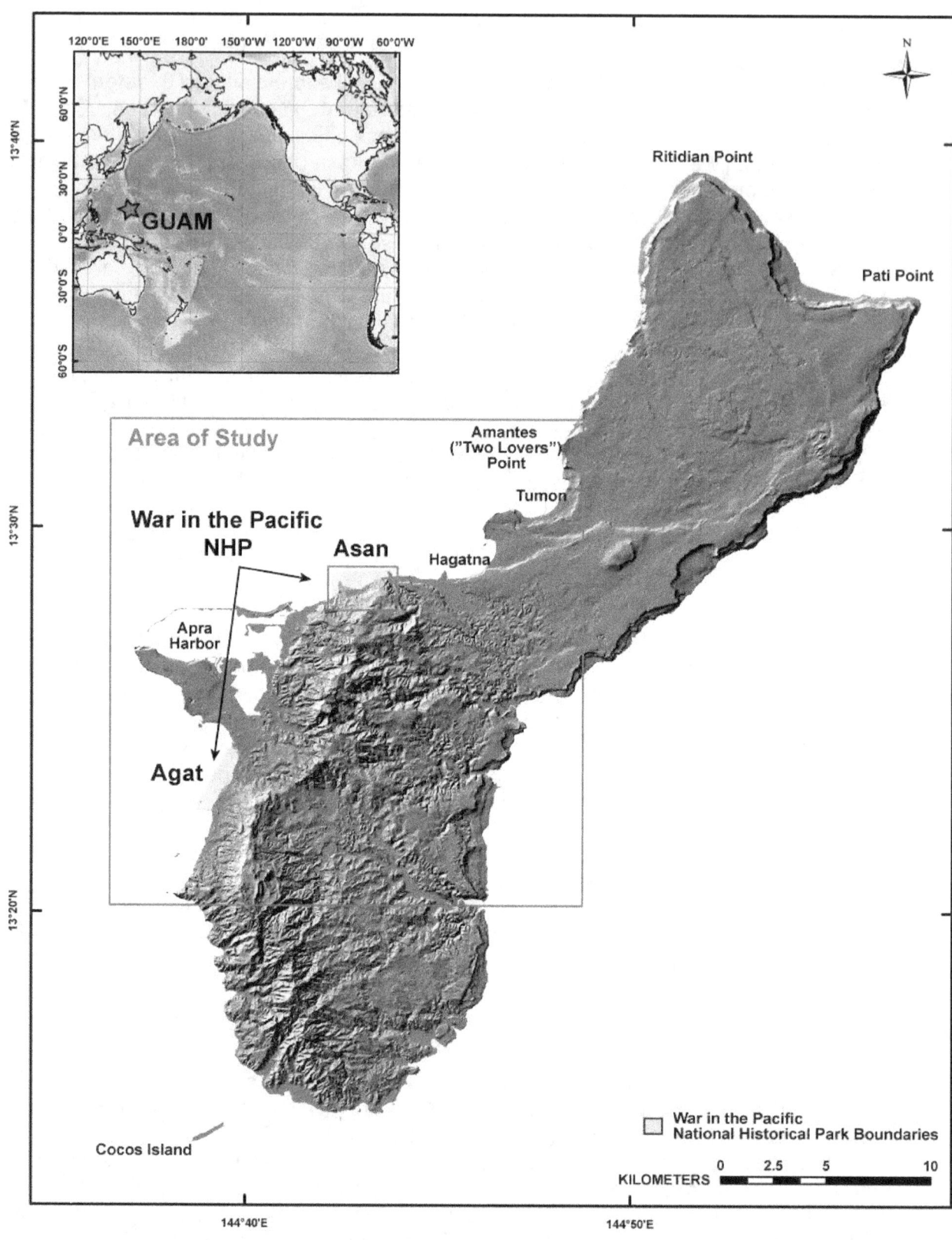

Figure 1. Map of Guam and its location in the western Pacific Ocean. The red boxes denote the study area and the yellow areas denote War-in-the-Pacific National Historical Park (WAPA) boundaries.

more than 3,300 mm (Lander and Guard, 2003). The wet season runs from July through November (~70 percent rainfall), with the remaining months constituting the dry season (~30 percent rainfall). On longer time scales, rainfall is correlated with El Nino-Southern Oscillation (ENSO), with the period from the end of the ENSO year through the year following ENSO tending to be very dry. The greatest frequency of typhoons occurs between October and November, however, they can form throughout the year. On average, 3 tropical storms and 1 typhoon pass within 330km of Guam each year.

U.S. Army Corps of Engineers (USACE) Wave Information Studies (WIS) wind and wave hindcast data for west-central Guam (Coastal Hydraulic Laboratory, 2008) for the period from 1981-2004 show the dominance of the northeast trade winds on the general wind and wave climate for the study area. Winds are predominantly out of the east-northeast at speeds of approximately 12 m/s; similarly, waves are primarily out of the east-northeast and have mean heights on the order of 2 m. While the mean wind and wave climate is dominated by the northeast trade winds, the influence of typhoons passing close to Guam is evident in the directional distribution of high-speed winds and large waves. While their frequency of occurrence is low, the direction of the fastest winds speeds and largest waves are more uniformly distributed than the means dominated by the trade winds, with the fastest wind speeds and largest waves coming out of the south and southwest. The tides along west-central Guam are described by the Center for Operational Oceanographic Products and Services (2008) as microtidal, semidiurnal, with 2 uneven high tides and low tides each day; the mean tidal range is 0.49 m and the diurnal tidal range is 0.72 m. Mean sea levels are generally highest (+6.4 mm) during July and lowest (-6.9 mm) during December (Pacific Islands Global Climate Observing System, 2008).

The seafloor in WAPA's Asan units was mapped by NOAA's National Center for Coastal Ocean Science (2005) as predominantly a coral pavement with limited aggregate reef. By their definition, the habitat consists of a macroalgae-covered (10 to <50 percent) reef flat, macroalgae-covered (50 to <90 percent) reef crest, coral-covered (10 to <50 percent) fore reef, and turf-covered (10 to <50 percent) upper insular shelf with interspersed patches of unconsolidated sediment, primarily off the awa channel in the reef flat referred to as the Cut just offshore of the bay's central coast. The study area and design were chosen specifically to characterize coastal circulation, sediment flux, and sediment residence time in WAPA's Asan Unit, an area of concern to NPS, but due to the wave exposure along this coast and vessel traffic, compromises were made to ensure safe deployment and recovery of the deployed instruments.

# Operations

This section provides information about the personnel, equipment, and field operations used during the study. See table 1 for a list of personnel involved in the experiment and tables 2 through 15 for complete listings of instrument and deployment information.

The proposed study consisted of 3 instrument suites to provide an integrated understanding of circulation and sediment dynamics in WAPA's coastal waters: terrestrial instruments, bottom-mounted oceanographic instruments, and spatial hydrographic surveys.

The terrestrial instruments included a weather station sampling every half hour and a digital camera system imaging the study area several times a day. The camera system was deployed at the Asan overlook to get as wide a field of view as possible of the Park's waters. The weather station was deployed along the shoreline at Asan to measure wind speed and direction, barometric pressure, air temperature and rainfall to provide meteorologic forcing information. The USGS river gauge on the Asan River was destroyed in Typhoon Pongsona in 2002, thus the necessary river discharge data was lacking to correlate to the proposed measurements made in the Park's waters. The USGS, therefore, deployed pressure sensors at the Marine Corps Drive Bridge over the Asan River in Asan to measure river stage as a proxy estimate for discharge.

The bottom-mounted oceanographic instruments were deployed in a "T" formation in WAPA's Asan Unit, consisting of a cross-shore line extending offshore from the river mouth to connect with a line extending alongshore on the fore reef (fig. 2). The moorings were placed along the cross-shore line to provide *in situ* measurements of the vertical structure of temperature, salinity, and turbidity in the water column from temperature/salinity sensors and optical backscatter sensors, respectively. The bottom packages included temperature/salinity sensors and optical backscatter sensors to make near-bed measurements of these parameters, along with upward-looking acoustic Doppler current profilers, which made measurements of current speed, current direction, and acoustic backscatter throughout the water column; all of these oceanographic sensors collected 1 averaged sample every 10 min. The acoustic Doppler current profilers also provided directional wave information every 2 hours. Additionally, 2 wave and tide gauges were deployed upcoast and downcoast of the park to provide nondirectional wave and water level boundary conditions for a 3-dimensional hydrodynamic numerical model for west-central Guam's waters. All of the measurements were on the insular shelf in water depths less than 20 m.

In addition to these fixed, bottom-mounted, time-series measurements, repetitive spatial surveys of water column properties (variations in water temperature, salinity, turbidity, dissolved oxygen, photosynthetically-available radiation, and fluorescence with depth) were made at a number of stations approximately every km from Two Lover's Point at the northern end of Tumon Bay south to Agat Harbor (fig. 1). This larger-scale alongshore survey was supplemented with a higher-density survey of the same parameters within WAPA's Asan Unit's waters and within Apra Harbor to compare to the *in situ*, bottom-mounted, time-series measurements and separate quantitative measurements of the coral reef ecosystem's structure made by the NPS.

## Equipment and Data Review

### Acoustic Doppler Current Profilers (ADCP)

Four upward-looking acoustic Doppler current profilers (ADCP) were mounted on MiniPROBEs (fig. 3a) along the 20 m isobath in Asan Bay and used to sample 48 0.5-m bins from 1.15 m above the seafloor up to the surface for 87.5 s at 2 Hz every 10 min to allow calculation of tides (m), mean current speeds (m/s) and directions (°True), and higher frequency motions, such as internal tidal bores and nonlinear internal waves. An upward-looking ADCP mounted on a MiniPROBE (fig. 3b) at a depth of 10 m in Asan Bay's Cut sampled 20 0.5-m bins from 1.25 m above the seafloor up to the surface for 120 s at 2 Hz every 10 min. Directional wave data were recorded for 512 s at 2 Hz every 2 hours; these data included water depth (m), current speed (m/s), and current direction (°True) every 0.5 s to compute tides (m), significant wave height (m), dominant wave period (s), mean wave direction (°True), and directional spread (°). Acoustic backscatter data (dB) collected from the ADCPs for the current measurements also provide information on the particulates in the water column and are used as a qualitative measurement of turbidity. The sensor locations are listed in tables 2 and 3; complete sensor and processing information is listed in appendix 1.

### Wave and Tide Gauges (WTG)

Two wave and tide gauges (WTG; fig. 3c) were deployed along the 10 m isobath and used to collect water level data for 512 s at 2 Hz every hour to compute tides (m), significant wave

Figure 2. Aerial photograph and SHOALS lidar of Asan Bay with the locations of the instrument sites.

height (m), and dominant wave period (s). One WTG was deployed off Two Lover's Point at the northern end of Tumon Bay, and 1 WTG was deployed off Agat Harbor to the south of Apra Harbor and the Orote Peninsula, to provide nondirectional wave and water level boundary conditions for a 3-dimensional hydrodynamic numerical model for west-central Guam's waters. The sensor locations are listed in tables 2 and 3; complete sensor and processing information is listed in appendix 2.

## Conductivity and Temperature (CT)

Twelve conductivity and temperature (CT) sensors (fig. 3d) collected and averaged 4 samples every 5 min to measure water temperature (°C) and conductivity (S/m), from which salinity in Practical Salinity Units (PSU) was calculated. The rapid sampling rate was established in an attempt to record the transient freshwater plumes being advected past the instruments. The instrument locations in the Cut were chosen to determine the presence of freshwater discharge. Offshore instrument locations were selected to record the areal extent, mixing, and direction of the freshwater plumes with oceanic water and to correlate the plumes with current measurements at the offshore sites. The deeper sites along the 20 m isobath were used to record the extent of freshwater mixing and to determine if internal bores pumped deep water up into the WAPA's shallows. The sensor locations are listed in tables 2 and 3; complete sensor and processing information is listed in appendix 2.

## Turbidity Sensors (SLOBS)

Eight self-logging optical backscatter sensors (SLOBS; fig. 3d) collected 8 samples every 5 min to measure turbidity data in Nephelometric Turbidity Units (NTU). The SLOBSs on the MiniPROBEs were mounted above the ADCPs in order for the turbidity data to be correlated with co-located ADCP acoustic backscatter data as discussed below. The sensor locations are listed in tables 2 and 3; complete sensor information is listed in appendix 2.

## Light Sensors (LS)

Six light sensors (LS; fig. 3b) collected a sample of luminance data (lux) every 60 min. One LS was deployed on the weather station to provide incident surface illumination information. The data from the LSs mounted on the MiniPROBEs were subtracted from the data values obtained from the LS deployed on the weather station to determine changes in illumination at the seafloor due to water column properties. The sensor locations are listed in tables 2 and 3; complete sensor information is listed in appendix 2.

## Pressure Loggers (PL)

Two pressure loggers (PL; fig. 3e) collected a sample of pressure data (mb) every 30 min. One PL was deployed at the NPS Maintenance Facility to provide atmospheric pressure information; these data were subtracted from the data values obtained from the PL deployed in the portable well in the Asan River to determine river stage. The sensor locations are listed in tables 2 and 3; complete sensor information is listed in appendix 2.

## Weather Station (WS)

Meteorological data was acquired by a self-contained weather station (WS) deployed on top of the old NPS library roof (fig. 3f), 17 m above ground, on the coast in central Asan. The WS recorded 25 min averages of barometric pressure (mb), air temperature (°C), precipitation (mm), wind speed (m/s), and wind direction (°True) every half hour. The instrument's location is listed in tables 2 and 3; complete sensor information is listed in appendix 3.

## Terrestrial Imaging System (TIS)

Imagery of the WAPA Asan Unit's hillslopes and coastal waters was collected using the USGS terrestrial imaging system (TIS), which consists of a Nikon CoolPix 8700 8-megapixel digital camera, a control unit, and battery in a waterproof housing with an external solar panel; both the housing and the solar panel were mounted on a vertical pole just below WAPA's Asan Bay overlook (fig. 3g). This system was employed to collect a time series of images to provide information on the natural frequency and duration of processes impacting the Asan Unit's hillslopes (rainfall, fire, and such) and Asan Bay (river discharge, freshwater plumes, sediment plumes, and such). The TIS took images every 2 hours during daylight hours (0600, 0800, 1000, 1200, 1400, 1600, and 1800 Chamorro Standard Time [ChST]) throughout the deployments. The sensor location is listed in tables 2 and 3; complete sensor information is listed in appendix 3.

Figure 3. Photographs of the equipment used in the study. *A,* Example of MiniProbe with ADCP, SLOBS, and CT along the 20 m isobath at Adelup Point. *B,* Cut MiniProbe at 10 m in the Cut; *C,* DOBIE wave. *D,* Microcat and SLOBS 3 m below the surface on a subsurface mooring. *E,* CTD profiler. *F,* Weather station. *G,* Terrestial imaging system at WAPA overlook. *H,* River gauge in Asan River.

## Water Column Profiler

Surveys of water column properties were made using a conductivity/temperature/depth (CTD) Profiler with optical backscatter (OBS), photosynthetically-available radiation (PAR), dissolved oxygen (DO), and chlorophyll (fluorescence) sensors to collect vertical profiles of water temperature (°C), salinity (PSU), density ($kg/m^3$), turbidity (NTU), PAR (mE), DO (percent), and fluorescence ($mg/m^3$), as shown in fig. 3h. The profiler cast location and depth information is listed in table 4; complete sensor information and individual cast acquisition logs are listed in appendixes 4-7. The profile surveys were conducted between Two Lover's Point and Agat Harbor and were repeated during 3 different seasons (July-wet, November-transitional, and February-dry).

## Sediment Data

Sediment traps were deployed during the second deployment (November 2007-January 2008) to collect suspended sediment from the water column. Simple tube traps, consisting of a clear plastic tube 60-cm long with an internal diameter of 6.7 cm, were deployed with their openings 0.7 m above the seabed at the six main instrument sites. A baffle was placed in the top of each tube trap to reduce turbulence and minimize disturbance by aquatic organisms (Bothner and others, 2006), as shown in fig. 3b. These standard USGS simple tube traps were used in this study for 2 reasons. First, in conjunction with the baffles, they provide the greater than 10:1 length-to-diameter ratio suggested for sediment traps (for example, Gardner and others, 1983; Baker and others, 1988) that is needed to minimize the effect of flow at the top of the trap, which causes eddies to propagate down into the trap and resuspend the trapped material. Secondly, the use of these standard traps allowed for comparison to other USGS sediment trap studies conducted elsewhere (for example, Bothner and others, 2006).

Because of the energetics of the inner shelf environment, the traps did not measure net vertical sediment flux to the coral reef surface. This is because material falling into the trap has a much lower potential for resuspension than the same material that settles on the adjacent reef surface (Bothner and others, 2006). In addition, the traps were likely to preferentially collect coarser particle sizes because of their higher settling velocity than finer particles. Particles with slow settling velocities relative to the circulation and exchange of water contained in the trap can be underrepresented in the collected samples (for example, Gardner and others, 1983; Baker and others, 1988). The location and depth information for the tube traps is listed in table 5. In addition to these suspended sediment samples, sea floor sediment samples were collected by divers at 3 of the five main study sites- there was insufficient sea floor sediment off Camel Rock and Adelup Point for samples. The bulk grain sizes of the sediment samples were analyzed using both Beckman Coulter Counter (silt and clay fractions) and 2 m settling tubes (sand fraction), and within each grain size fraction the percent carbonate was determined with a UIC Coulometer. The carbonate and terrigenous percentages for the sand-, silt-, and clay-size fractions were determined using the methodology developed by Barber (2002).

## Miscellaneous Data Sources

The far-field meteorologic forcing for the study period was compiled by NCDC's (2008) Andersen Air Force Base Guam weather station. This station collected hourly measurements of barometric pressure (mb), wind speed (m/s), wind direction (°True), and air temperature (°C). Navigation equipment for deployment, recovery, and survey operations included hand-held WAAS-equipped GPS units and a computer with positioning and mapping software. The positioning and mapping software enabled real-time GPS position data to be combined with images of previously collected high-resolution SHOALS color-coded LiDAR, shaded-relief bathymetry, 5 m isobaths, and aerial photographs of terrestrial portions of the maps.

## Numerical Circulation Modeling

A Delft3D coupled 3-dimensional, wave-current numerical circulation model of Asan Bay was constructed in order to extrapolate the limited Eulerian point measurements spatially and to examine the effects of waves, winds, and tides on circulation and buoyant transport over WAPA's coral reef ecosystem. The main components of the model are the coupled Delft3D-Wave and Delft3D-Flow modules, and a steering module (MORSYS) describing the sequence of alternating calls between waves and flow. Delft3D-Flow forms the core of the model system and simulates water motion due to tidal and meteorological forcing by solving the unsteady shallow-water equations that consist of the continuity equation, the horizontal momentum equations, and the transport equation under the shallow water and Boussinesq assumptions. Vertical accelerations are assumed minor compared to gravitational acceleration (shallow water assumption), thus reducing the vertical momentum equation to the hydrostatic pressure relation. By specifying boundary conditions for bed roughness (quadratic friction law), free surface (wind stress), lateral boundaries (water level and currents) and closed boundaries with free-slip conditions at the coasts, the equations can be solved on a staggered grid by using an Alternating Direction Implicit method (Stelling 1984; Leendertse, 1987, Delft User Manual, 2006).

Wave effects, such as enhanced bed shear stresses and wave-induced current forcing due to wave breaking, are integrated in the flow simulation by running the 3rd generation SWAN wave processor (Version 40.41A). The SWAN-model is based on discrete spectral action balance equations, computing the evolution of random, short-crested waves (Holthuijsen and others, 1993; Booij and others, 1999; Ris, 1999). Physical processes include generation of waves by wind, dissipation due to whitecapping, bottom friction and depth-induced breaking, and, nonlinear quadruplet and triad wave-wave interactions. Wave propagation, growth, and decay are solved periodically on subsets of the flow grid. The results of the wave simulation, such as wave height, peak spectral period, and mass fluxes are stored on the computational flow grid and included in the flow calculations through additional driving terms near the surface and bed, enhanced bed shear stress, mass flux, and increased turbulence (for example, Walstra and others, 2000).

## Research Platform and Field Operations

The instrument deployments and recoveries were conducted using the *F/V Heavy Metal*. Vessel operations, including mobilization and demobilization, were based out of Hagatna boat basin and Agat marina. The port quarterdeck was adapted for instrument deployment and recovery operations, which included the use of an electric winch and an overhead davit. The instruments were deployed by attaching a removable bridle to the instrument package with a connecting line through the davit and down to the winch. The instruments were lowered to within a few meters of the seafloor where scuba divers attached a lift bag and detached the lifting line. The divers then moved the instrument package into position for anchoring. Surficial seafloor sediment samples were collected, and the heights of the sensors above the seafloor were measured and recorded. Recovery operations employed the same techniques. The water column profiler casts were conducted by hand from the same vessel. The driver's station was outfitted with a laptop computer and GPS-enabled navigation system to provide the vessel captain with a graphic display of position information, speed, heading and distance to the next location.

# Data Acquisition and Quality

Data were acquired for 185 days during the periods from July 23, 2007, to October 25, 2007, and from November 5, 2007, through January 30, 2008 (2007 Year Day [YD] 204-298 and 309-395), with a period of instrument recovery and refurbishment from XX-YY. More than 6,600,000 data points were recorded by the ADCPs, CTs, SLOBSs, WTGs, LSs, PLs, and WS; more than 40,000 data points were recorded by the water column profiler; and 1,364 images were taken by the TIS. The raw data were archived and copies of the data were post-processed for analysis.

The ADCP, CT, PL, and weather station data generally appeared to be of high quality. In order to determine the contributions of different forcing mechanisms to flow patterns, the current data were constrained to periods when just the forcing mechanism was dominant. For example, in order to identify the influence of trade winds (large waves) on flow patterns, a period of time was identified without concurrent large waves (strong trade winds), and the data were 36-hour low-pass filtered to remove the influence of tides; to identify the contribution of tides, a period of time without trade winds or large waves was selected and then 10-28 hour band-pass filtered.

The SLOBS and LS data were severely degraded due to biofouling and inadequate cleaning, limiting their datasets to a few days to weeks at a time. In order to extend the limited turbidity data, the turbidities recorded by the SLOBS during non-biofouled periods were correlated to co-located ADCP acoustic backscatter data that had already been processed for beam spreading and attenuation using the methodology proposed by Deines (1999). The resulting regression equations were then used to estimate NTU values from the corrected acoustic backscatter data throughout the rest of the deployments when biofouling impaired the SLOBS data.

The TIS imagery, while overall very good, was slightly degraded toward the end of the first deployment (July 2007-November 2007) due to the growth of a plant into the camera's field of view. The water column profiler data were very high in quality; as typical, the data near the seabed often displayed spikes in the OBS data due to interaction of the optical beam with the seabed.

# Results

This section reviews the data collected by the instruments during the deployments and addresses the significance of the findings to better understand the oceanographic conditions in the study area.

## Oceanographic and Atmospheric Forcing

The study period from July 2007 through January 2008 covered 2 distinct seasons: the wet rainy season that normally runs from July through November, and the dry trade-wind season that normally runs from December through June. The transition during our study period occurred around Year Day 335 (December 1, 2007) as shown in the meteorological data in fig. 4. At the beginning of the study the wind speeds and directions measured at Andersen Air Force Base (AAFB; at Pati Point in fig. 1) and at the weather station along Asan Bay (WS, fig. 2) were variable in strength and duration, although consistently stronger at the more exposed AAFB (fig. 4c,d). The transition to the dry season was marked by more consistent wind speeds and directions from the northeast at both AAFB and the Asan WS, again with higher speeds at AAFB (fig. 4c,d).

Rainfall during the study period followed the seasonal trends with greater rainfall during the wet season, and a higher frequency at the Asan WS than at AAFB, potentially due to topographic variations. The hourly precipitation ranged from 0.0 to 25.3 mm, with a mean rainfall ± 1 standard deviation of 0.1±0.8 mm (table 6). The air temperature also followed the seasonal trend with warmer and more variable temperatures during the wet season that transitioned to cooler, more consistent temperatures in the dry season (fig. 4b). The air temperature ranged from 23.94 to 36.50°C with a mean temperature ± 1 standard deviation of 27.71±2.13°C.

## River Discharge

A pressure sensor was deployed 70 m upstream from the Asan River's mouth to provide a relative measurement of water level and discharge (fig. 4f); the river's mouth was generally closed due to the presence of a river-mouth bar that caused a small estuary to form. Water levels at the pressure sensor ranged from 0.36 to 1.04 m, with a mean ± 1 standard deviation of 0.46±0.10 m. The water levels were a function of local precipitation and the breaching of the river-mouth bar. Water levels reached their maximum elevations when the precipitation generated runoff and river discharge, but the river-mouth bar was sufficiently high to contain the water in the small bar-built estuary. When the precipitation and river discharge were great enough to breach the bar (as occurred on YD 221), or when ocean waves eroded the seaward side of the bar (as occurred on YD 377), the water levels rapidly dropped as the pent-up waters discharged into Asan Bay.

## Tides

The study period encompassed more than 11 complete spring-neap tidal cycles. The tides in Asan Bay are microtidal, mixed, semidiurnal with 2 uneven high tides and 2 uneven low tides per day; thus, the tides change just over every 6 hours (fig. 5a). The mean daily tidal range was approximately 0.71 m, while the minimum and maximum daily tidal ranges were 0.16 and 1.10 m during neap and spring tides, respectively.

## Winds

The winds speeds at the WAPA ranged from 0.00 to 8.25 m/s, with a mean speed ± 1 standard deviation of 1.53±0.87 m/s during the deployment (table 6). Wind speeds measured in the southern end of Asan Bay were slightly lower but more consistent during the winter months (fig. 5b, YD 330-390) than the wet season months (fig. 5b, YD 210-330) due to the passage of storm systems. The topography and location of the anemometer at the WAPA WS may have resulted in lower wind speeds during the dry season in comparison to AAFB where the sensor was more exposed to open ocean conditions.

## Currents

The mean current speed at the 4 deep (20 m water depth) MiniProbe sites ± 1 standard deviation for Asan Bay during the study period was 0.12±0.05 m/s close to the surface and 0.06±0.03 m/s close to the sea floor (fig. 5c, table 7). The greater near surface current speeds during the dry season were likely a result of more consistent trade-wind forcing.

Red = War in the Pacific National Historical Park        Blue = Andersen Air Force Base

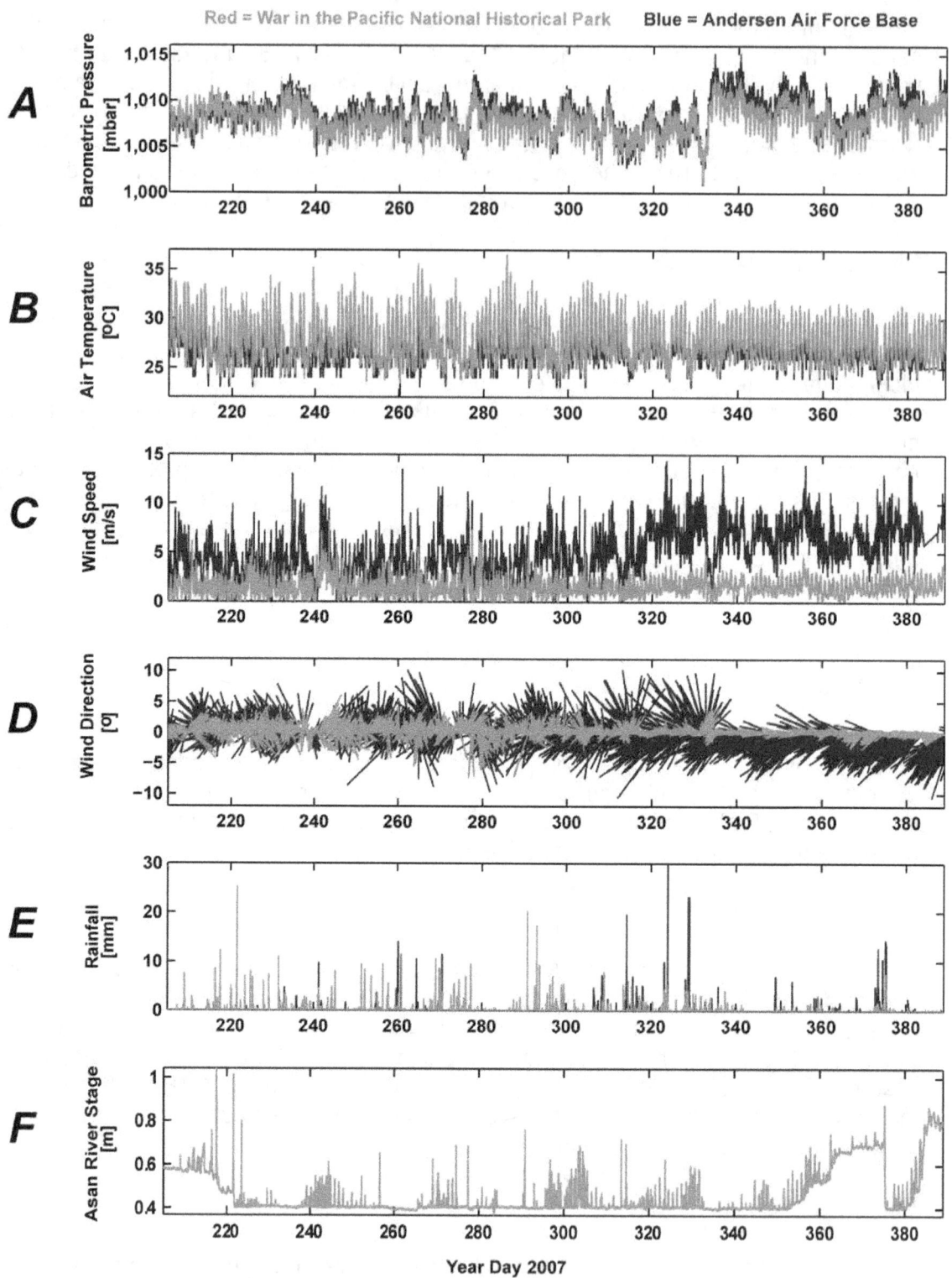

Figure 4. Meteorological forcing data during the study period from the War-in-the-Pacific National Historical Park (WAPA, red), and Andersen Air Force Base (blue), weather stations. *A*, Barometric pressure, in millibars. *B*, Air temperature, in degrees Celsius. *C*, Wind speed, in meters per second. *D*, Wind speed and direction, in meters per second from degrees true north. *E*, Rainfall, in millimeters. *F*, Asan River stage (water level), in meters. The meterologic data shows the transition from the warm, rainy season to the drier, windier, and cooler season beginning around 2007 Year Day 335 (December 1, 2007).

## Waves

The waves that impacted WAPA during the course of the experiment are shown in fig. 5d,e. Significant wave heights ranged from 0.23 to 2.31 m, with a mean significant height ± 1 standard deviation of 0.72±0.28 m (table 8). Dominant wave periods varied from 3 to 11.2 s, with a mean dominant period ± 1 standard deviation of 5.78±1.11 s. The mean wave direction ± 1 standard deviation was 344.8±37.7°. The first deployment from YD 204-298 (July 2007–October 2007) was relatively quiescent, except for 1 large wave event from YD 279-282, when waves with heights greater than 2 m and periods of 10 s were measured. Consistently larger waves (>1 m) were observed throughout the trade wind dominated second deployment (November 2007–January 2008).

## Temporal Variations Water Column Properties

The water column properties that were measured by the deployed CTs and SLOBS included variations in temperature (°C), salinity (PSU), and suspended sediment concentrations (mg/L). The water column properties that were measured by the CTD/OBS/PAR profiler included variations in temperature (°C), salinity (PSU), turbidity (NTU), PAR (mE), DO (percent), and chl (mg/m$^3$) with depth.

### Temperature

Water temperatures ranged between 27.03 and 34.21°C, with a mean temperature ± 1 standard deviation of 29.6±0.32°C (table 9). The water typically warmed 1 to 2°C at the shallow sites during the day due to insolation (fig. 6b), while the variability at the deep sites appeared to be related to tidal forcing, with frequent rapid decreases in water temperature on the order of 1 to 4°C (fig. 6d); this same change in water temperature due to the tides may have occurred at the shallow sites but is masked by the diurnal warming trend. A seasonal shift to decreased variability in temperature at the deep sites was observed around YD 335 that coincided with a seasonal shift in wind speed and direction (fig. 7a,c).

### Salinity

Salinity in the bay ranged between 30.77 and 34.88 PSU, with a mean salinity ± 1 standard deviation of 34.01±0.22 PSU (table 10). Salinity at the shallow sites was fairly constant at approximately 34 PSU, with slight dips during precipitation and corresponding river flood events (fig. 6c). Salinity at the Cut Edge site followed the same general trend as the other shallow sites but was much lower, likely due to either greater surface freshwater percolating through the Asan River mouth's bar or to submarine groundwater discharge in this area. Salinity at the deeper sites was slightly higher than at the shallow sites due to the influence of saltier oceanic water, although these sites did experience a decrease in salinity during times of heavy precipitation (fig. 6e, days 285-300).

### Turbidity

Concurrent, reliable turbidity data were recorded for only 16 days from YD 208-225 (July 28-August 13, 2007) from the SLOBS instruments. During that time period, the turbidity in the

15

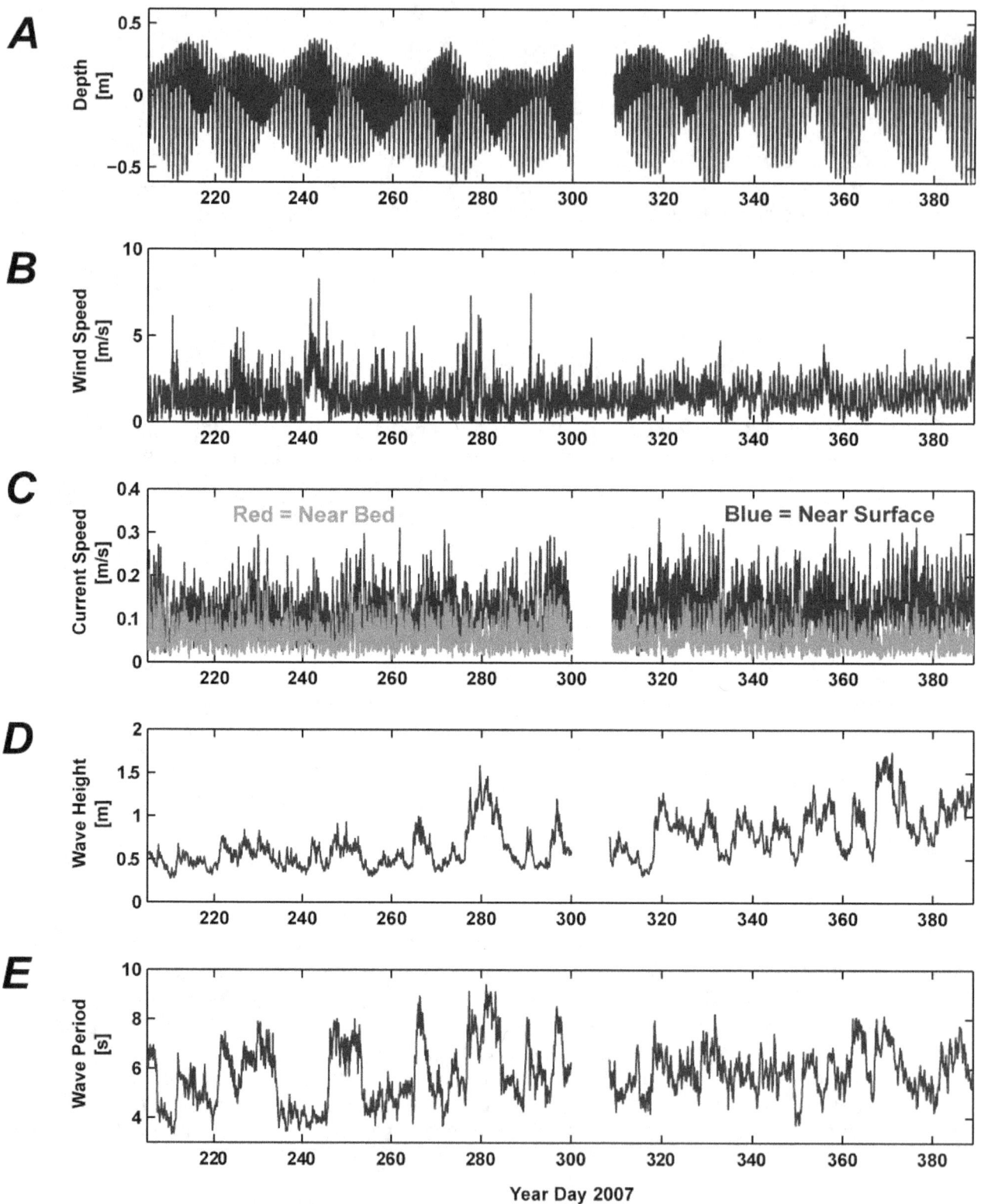

Figure 5. Oceanographic data for the entire study period. *A,* Tide, in meters. *B,* Wind speed, in meters per second. *C,* Mean current speed, in meters per second. *D,* Mean wave height, in meters. *E,* Mean wave period, in seconds. The oceanographic data shows the seasonality and influence of locality on wind speed, currents, and waves. The gap in the data records between 2007 Year Days 300-308 denotes the period when the instruments were out of the water between deployments for refurbishment.

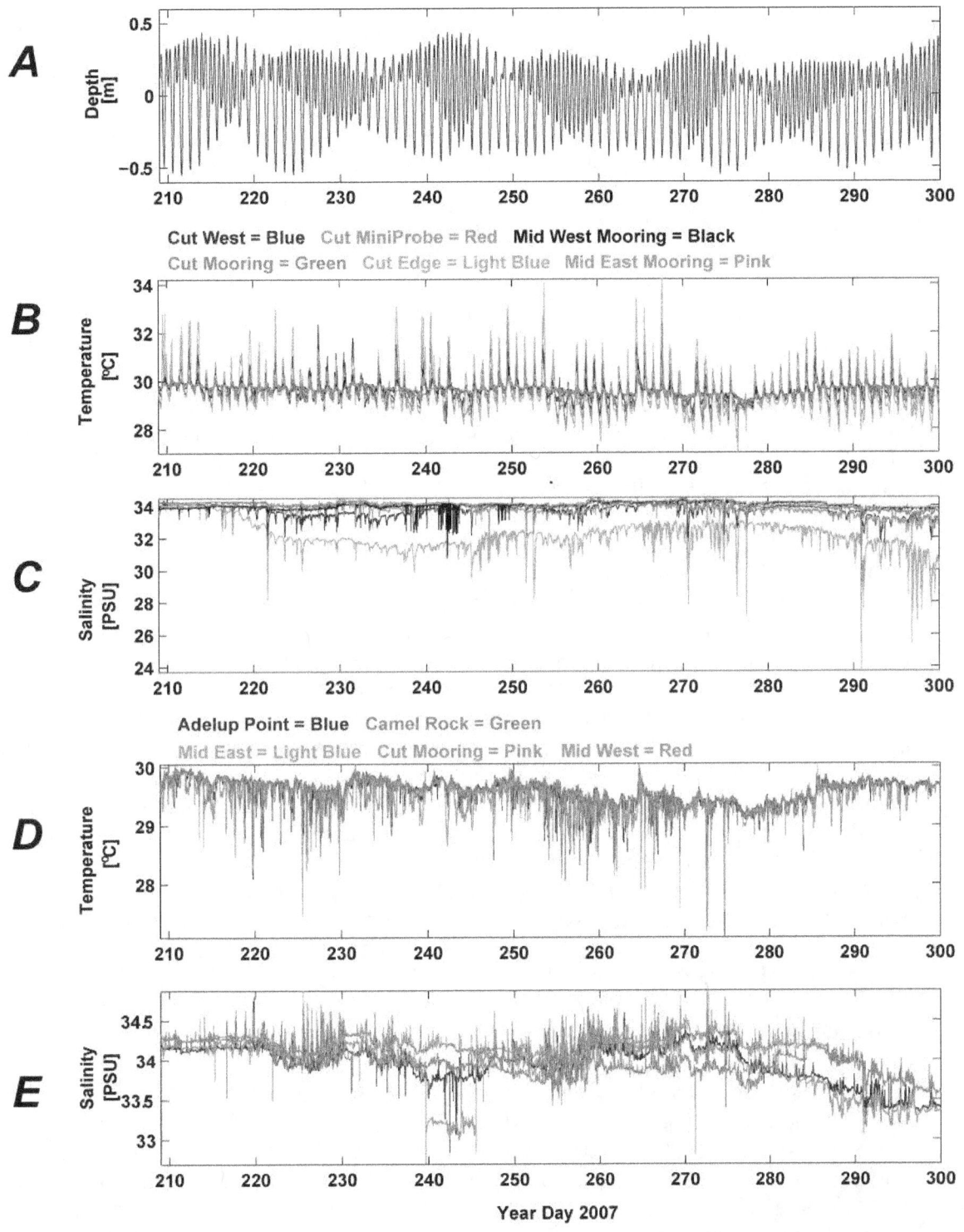

Figure 6. Tide, temperature, and salinity for the shallow and deep sites. *A,* Tide, in meters. *B,* Temperature at the shallow sites, in degrees Celsius. *C,* Salinity at the shallow sites, in Practical Salinity Units. *D,* Temperature at the deep sites, in degrees Celsius. *E,* Salinity at the deep sites, in Practical Salinity Units. The data at the shallow sites show daily variability due to tides and increases of 1 to 4°C in temperature due primarily to insolation, while salinity is fairly constant with changes due to the tides and river discharge. The data from the deep sites show significant decreases in temperature and increases in salinity during falling tides due to internal motions that move colder, more saline water up onto the insular shelf.

study area ranged between 0.0 and 1,180.3 NTU, with a mean turbidity ± 1 standard deviation of 6.08±4.61 NTU (table 11). The acoustic backscatter data from the ADCPs provided a relative measure of turbidity in the bay during times of biofouling of the SLOBS sensors. The near surface and near bed turbidity at the deep MiniProbe sites along the 20 m isobath were very low throughout the study (fig. 8, table 12). The Cut site showed the largest variability and highest relative turbidity values (fig. 8c). In general, turbidity was low and little variability was observed at the deep and shallow sites outside of the Cut (fig. 8).

## Spatial Variations in Water Column Properties

### West-Central Guam

Surveys of the water column were conducted from Tumon Bay south to Agat Harbor on the central west coast of Guam on 3 different days spanning the wet and dry seasons. These surveys provide insight into the physical structure of the water column along 35 km of west-central Guam's shoreline and are useful for putting the high-resolution measurements made in WAPA's Asan Unit into regional context.

The July 2007 survey showed constant salinity with lower salinity areas near Tumon and Hagatna Bays (fig. 9). The temperatures in July were the warmest of the 3 surveys and show relatively consistent values through the entire water column to depths of 20 m. The turbidity values during this survey were relatively low, except in the areas of Tumon and Haganta Bay, similar to the salinity profiles. PAR, DO, and chl were highly variable.

The second survey in November 2007 showed lower salinity overall than the July survey, potentially due to the increase in precipitation between the 2 periods. Temperatures were slightly cooler, likely due to the change in seasons, and were fairly uniform through the water column. The turbidity during this survey was also low, with a few regions of high turbidity north of Tumon Bay, between Tumon and Hagatna Bay, and between Hagatna and Asan Bay. Overall, the PAR, DO, and chl had higher values during the November survey (fig. 10). The final survey in February 2008 showed uniform salinity values with a slight decrease near Hagatna Bay. Overall, the salinity values were consistent with the prior surveys. The temperature values were the lowest of the 3 surveys due to lower insolation in the winter. The turbidity values, while in general lower than during the previous 2 surveys, were higher again in Asan Bay relative to the rest of the study area. PAR, DO, and chl were higher than the previous surveys (fig. 11).

### Asan Bay

The profiler surveys in Asan Bay provide greater spatial and vertical resolution than the long-term moored and bottom-mounted instruments. The July 2007 survey was at the beginning of the wet season that coincided with heavy precipitation. The July 2007 surveys (figs. 12-13) showed lower salinity, lower temperature, and higher turbidity waters at Asan Cut for up to 10 m below the sea surface and extending more than 800 m offshore. These values indicate that freshwater and sediment were being advected out of the Cut and transported offshore in a low-density plume. It appears that sediment was slowly settling from the plume, which extended down to more than 20 m depth at its offshore extent.

The profiler surveys from the November 2007 survey, which occurred during the transition from the wet to the dry season, showed a similar surface plume at Asan Cut with lower salinity, lower temperature, and higher turbidity (figs. 14-15). In general, the freshwater surface plume

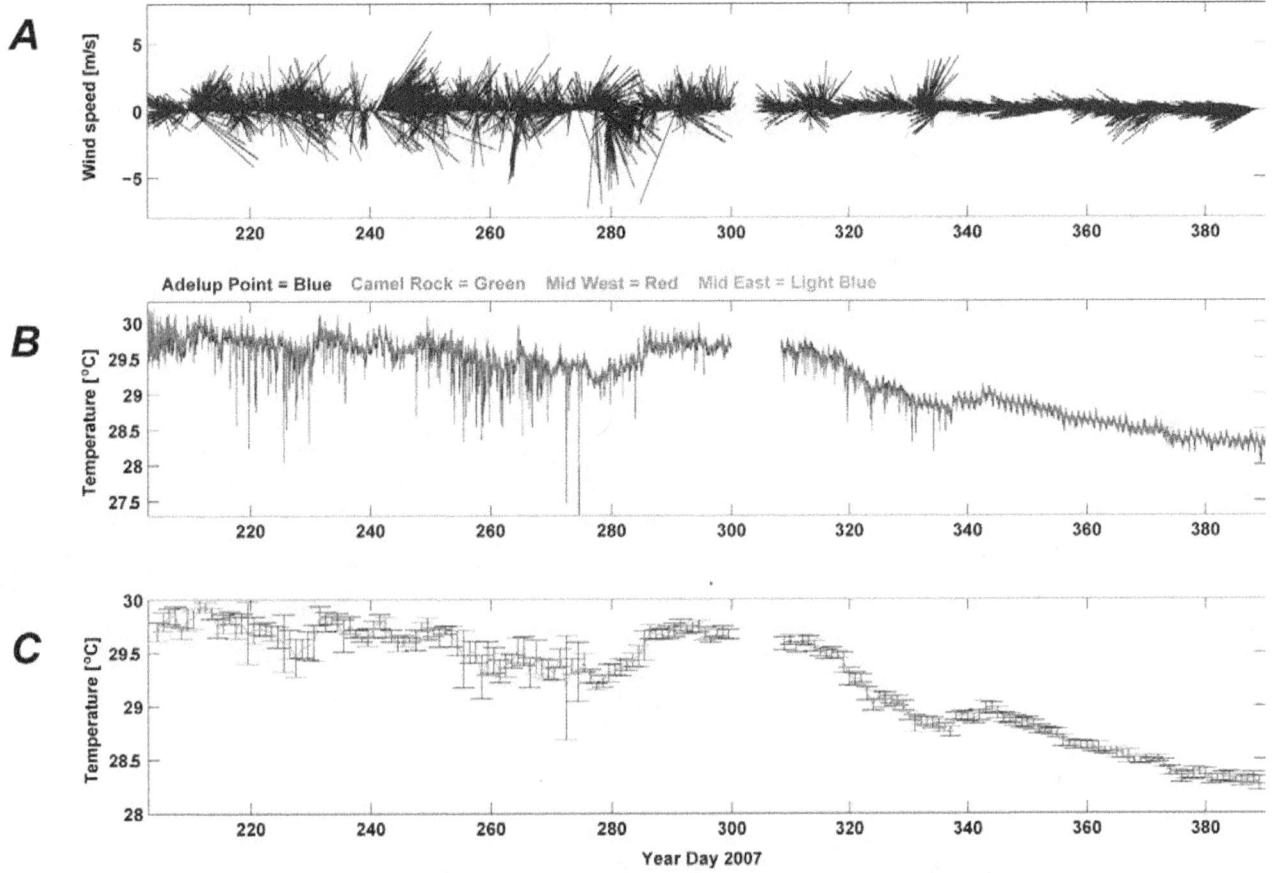

**Figure 7.** Temperature variability as a function of wind forcing. *A,* Wind speed and direction, in meters per second from degrees true north. *B,* Temperature, in degrees Celsius; *C,* Daily mean temperature and standard deviation, in degrees Celsius. The seasonal shift to more consistent wind speeds and directions correlates with the decrease in temperature variability during the deployment.

was more turbid and confined closer to the surface than during the previous survey. The shore-parallel survey shows low temperature and high salinity values in a 10 m-thick wedge above the bottom at Adelup Point. This wedge of higher salinity and lower temperature water at greater depths is consistent with the time series observations that showed the anomalous salinity and temperature values at the deep sites likely related to internal tidal motions.

The shore parallel survey from February 2008 during the dry season shows a much smaller freshwater and turbidity plume at Asan Cut (figs. 16-17), presumably because the drier conditions during this survey resulted in less turbid and freshwater entering the bay. The salinity and temperature profiles show warmer, fresher water at the surface and cooler, more saline water at depth, while the profiles to the east and west of Asan Cut are relatively uniform in temperature and salinity with depth. Higher turbidity was observed only at the surface near Asan Cut. The shore-normal profile also shows the freshwater and turbid plume were confined to the surface (top meter) and extended approximately 300 m offshore.

## Sediment

As shown in table 5, most of the sediment trap collection rates to the east and west of the Cut were rather low (4.77-6.30 mg/cm$^2$/day). In the Cut, however, the trap collection rate

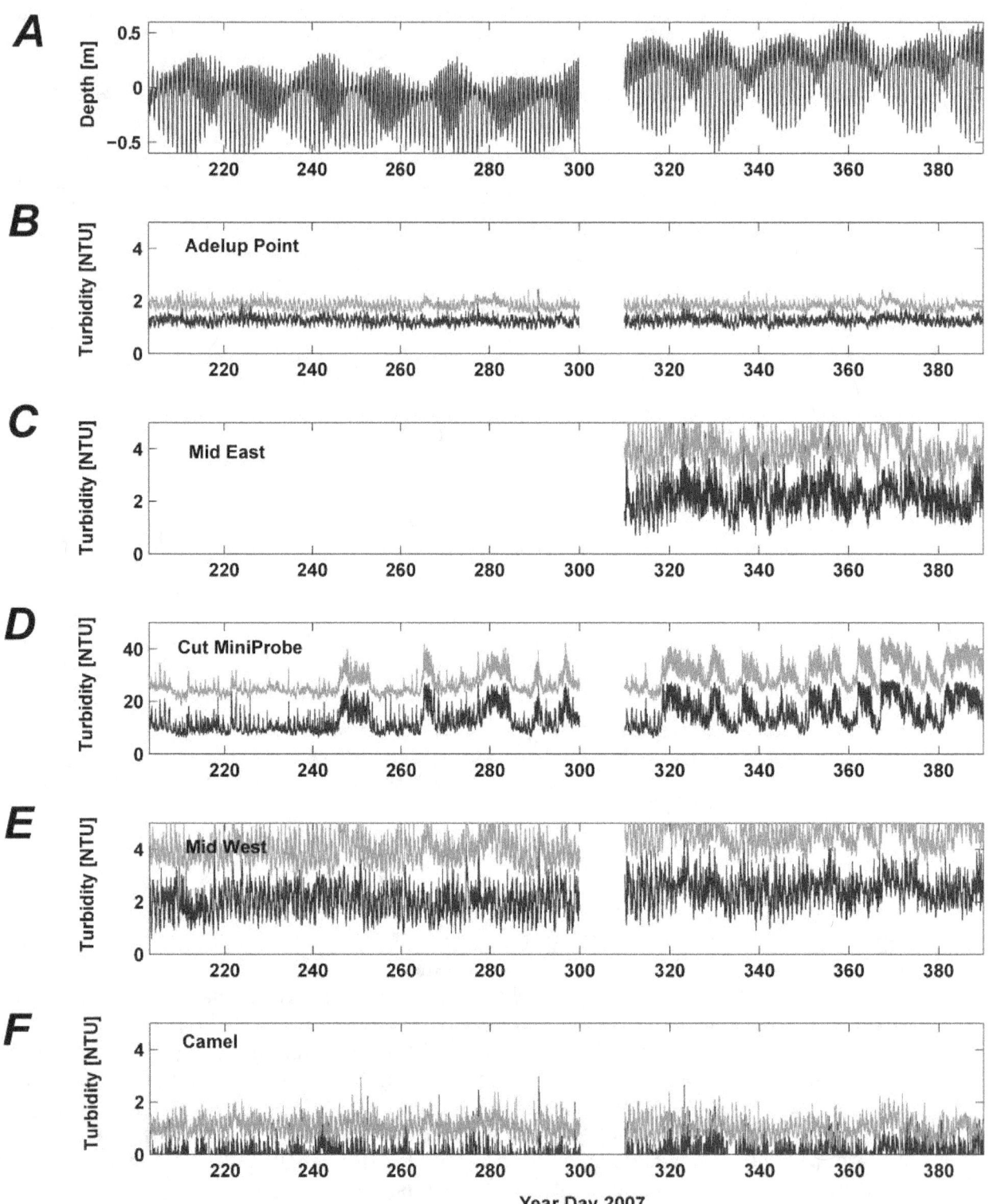

**Figure 8.** Tide and turbidity data near the bed (red), and near the surface (blue), at the MiniProbe sites, from east to west. *A,* Tide, in meters. *B,* Turbidity at Adelup Point, in Nephelometric Turbidity Units. *C,* Turbidity at Mid East MiniProbe, in Nephelometric Turbidity Units. *D,* Turbidity at Asan Cut MiniProbe, in Nephelometric Turbidity Units. *E,* Turbidity at Mid West MiniProbe, in Nephelometric Turbidity Units. *F,* Turbidity at Camel Rock MiniProbe, in Nephelometric Turbidity Units. Turbidity was highest near the Cut and progressively lower with distance offshore at the other sites.

approached 70 mg/cm$^2$/day, potentially resulting in mortality of adult corals (Phillips and Fabricius, 2003). The sea floor and sediment trap samples from the same locations differed both by grain size and composition. All of the sea floor sediment samples were gravely sands, with less than 5 percent mud (silts+clays; fig. 18a; table 14). In contrast, the sediment trap samples, including the ones deployed at the sites where the sea floor samples were taken, were predominantly sandy muds, except for those in the Cut, which were muddy sands (fig. 18b). This difference in grain size between the sea floor and what accumulates in sediment traps is not uncommon, for finer-grained, lighter particles can be more easily resuspended and carried higher up into the water column and, thus, to the height of the trap's opening than coarser particles and settle more slowly than coarser particles. Once these fine-grained particles settle into the trap, they cannot be resuspended and advected away as could the same-sized material on the adjacent sea floor. Furthermore, as discussed above, the sediment traps preferentially collect coarser particle sizes because of their higher settling velocity than finer particles.

All of the sea floor sediment samples were predominantly (82-93 percent) reef-derived calcium carbonate, with 10-11 percent total inorganic carbon and 7-18 percent terrigenous material (fig. 19a; table 15). In contrast, the sediment trap samples, including the 1s deployed at the sites where the sea floor samples were taken, were predominantly (65-85 percent) terrigenous material and, to a lesser extent, calcium carbonate (15-35 percent) and total inorganic carbon (2-4 percent). The Cut Mooring site and Cut MiniProbe site, however, consisted of mostly carbonate material (58-60 percent), more than a third terrigenous material (40-42 percent), and approximately 7 percent inorganic carbon (fig. 19b).

## Numerical Circulation Model

The Delft3D coupled wave-current numerical circulation model settings for the 4 model runs are presented in table 16. A total of 11 model runs were performed, with the first seven runs comprising model development and refinement. With the model in good working order, 4 model runs (table 17) were conducted to explore the influence of different sets of wave conditions (small, short-period trade-wind waves and larger, longer-period swells from different directions) under constant trade-wind forcing and tide data collected as part of the field experiment. All of the model runs were conducted over a 24-hour period in order to encompass a complete mixed, semidiurnal tidal cycle; the results presented show the net flow during the model run.

In the model runs with waves out of the northeast (figs. 20-21), wave breaking is concentrated on the east-facing portions of the reef crest and minimal on the eastern side of the Cut. These patterns of wave breaking drive flow shoreward across the reef crest onto the reef flat, where currents are strongly to the west along the eastern half of the reef flat and weaker to the east along the western half of the reef flat, converging into the Cut. Thus, it appears that wind- and wave-driven flow up onto the reef flat is balanced by offshore-directed return flow out of the Cut. This return flow is then driven to the northwest and west upon exiting the Cut, primarily due to wave-driven flow over the fore reef. There appears to be a small recirculation eddy in the lee of the northwestward-flowing return flow draining the reef flat that likely may help to retain buoyant or dissolved material. The difference between the wave breaking and flow patterns due to larger storm waves (fig. 20) and smaller trade-wind waves (fig. 21) is in the greater fraction of breaking at the reef crest, resulting in faster current speeds on the reef flat during the larger storm waves than during trade wind-wave forcing.

In the model runs with waves out of the northwest (figs. 22-23), wave breaking is concentrated on the west-facing portions of the reef crest and minimal on the western side of the

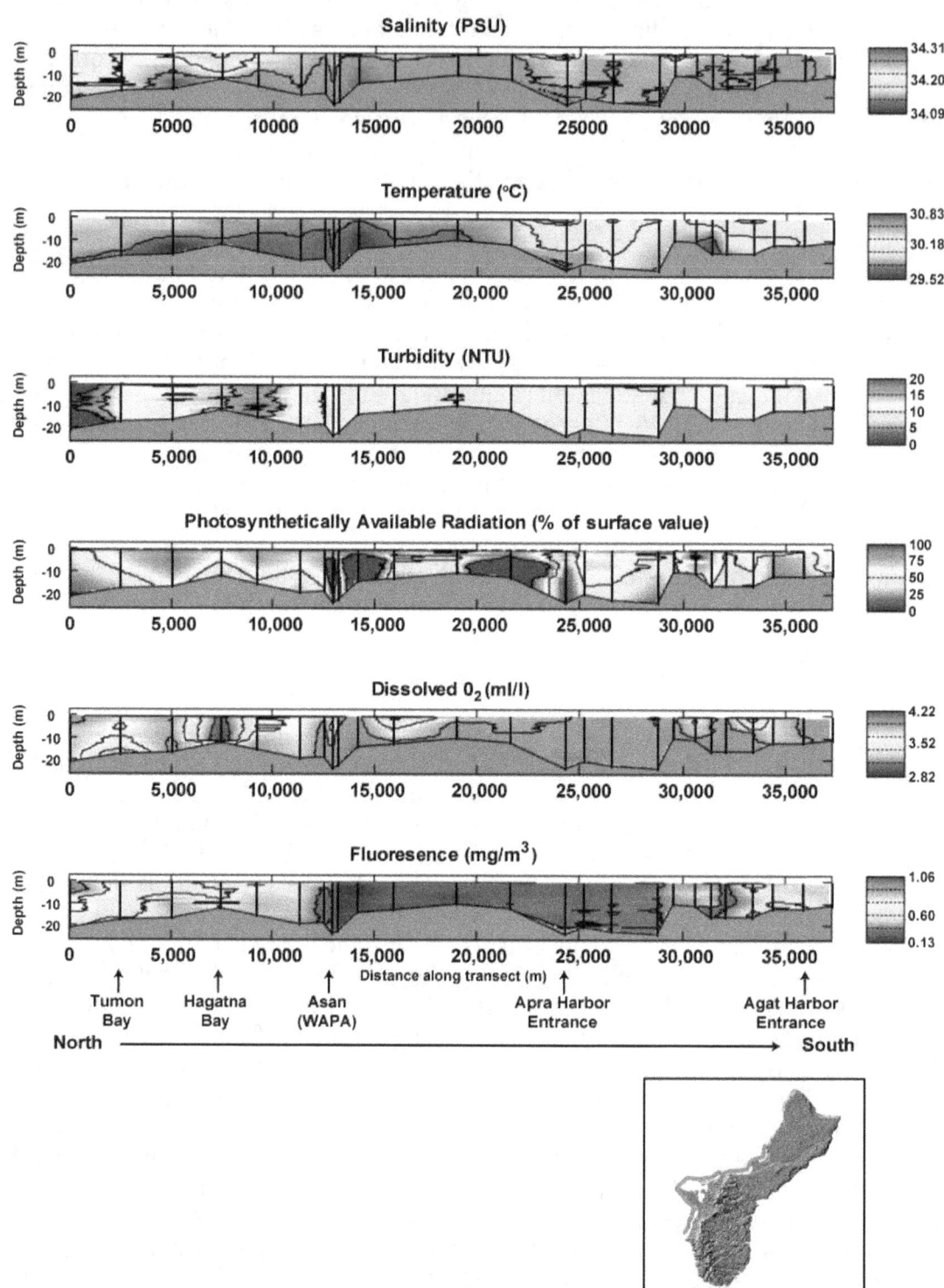

Figure 9. Alongshore variability in water column properties off west-central Guam in July 2007. *A,* Salinity, in Practical Salinity Units. *B,* Temperature, in degrees Celsius. *C,* Turbidity, in Nephelometric Turbidity Units. *D,* Photosynthetically-available radiation, in percent of surface value. *E,* Dissolved oxygen, in milliliters per liter. *F,* Fluorescence, in milligrams per cubic meter. Note the high variability both within the water column at a given location and alongshore between sites.

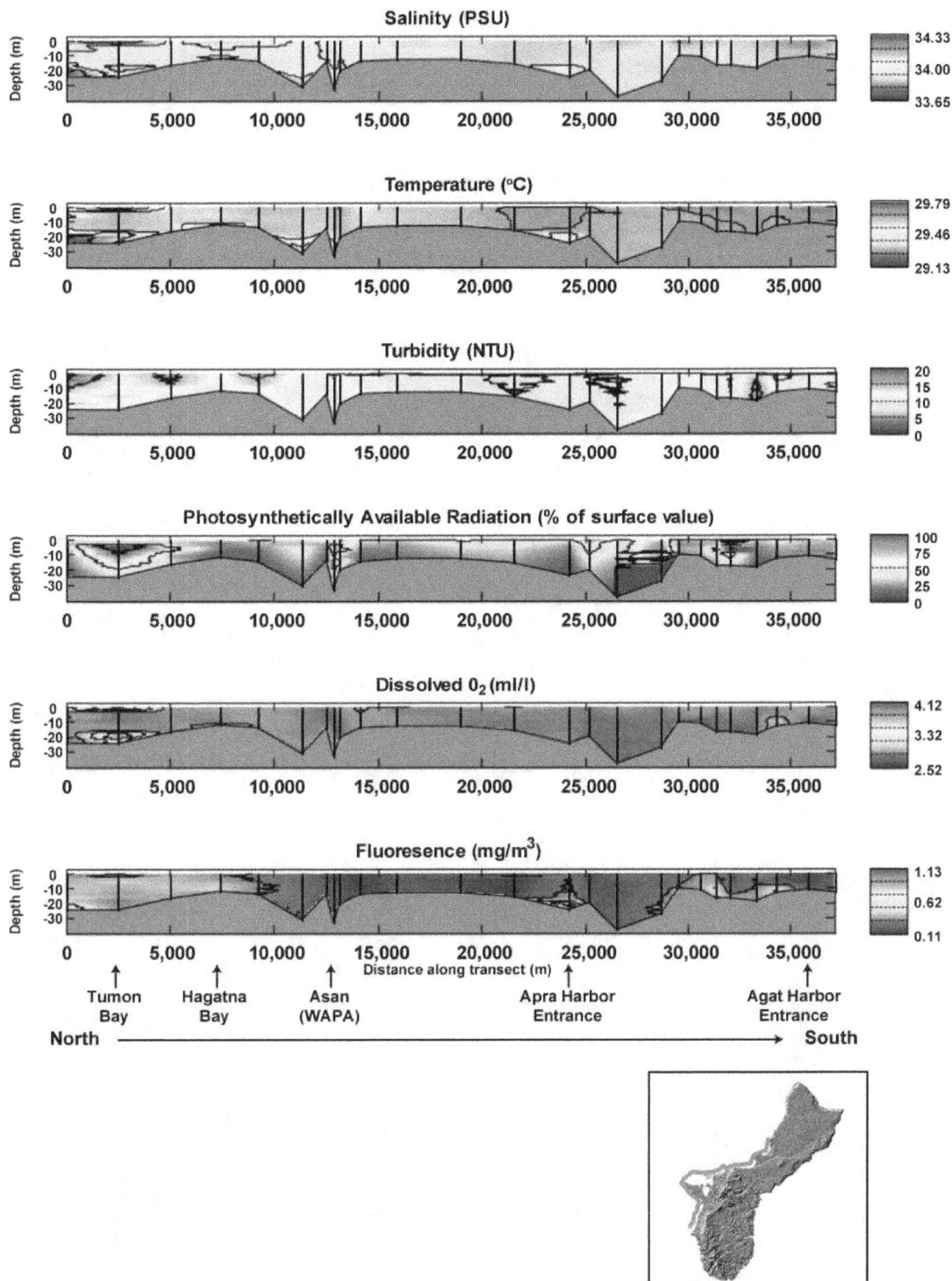

**Figure 10.** Alongshore variability in water column properties off west-central Guam in November 2007. *A,* Salinity, in Practical Salinity Units. *B,* Temperature, in degrees Celsius. *C,* Turbidity, in Nephelometric Turbidity Units. *D,* Photosynthetically-available radiation, in percent of surface value. *E,* Dissolved oxygen, in milliliters per liter. *F,* Fluorescence, in milligrams per cubic meter. Note the high variability both within the water column at a given location and alongshore between sites.

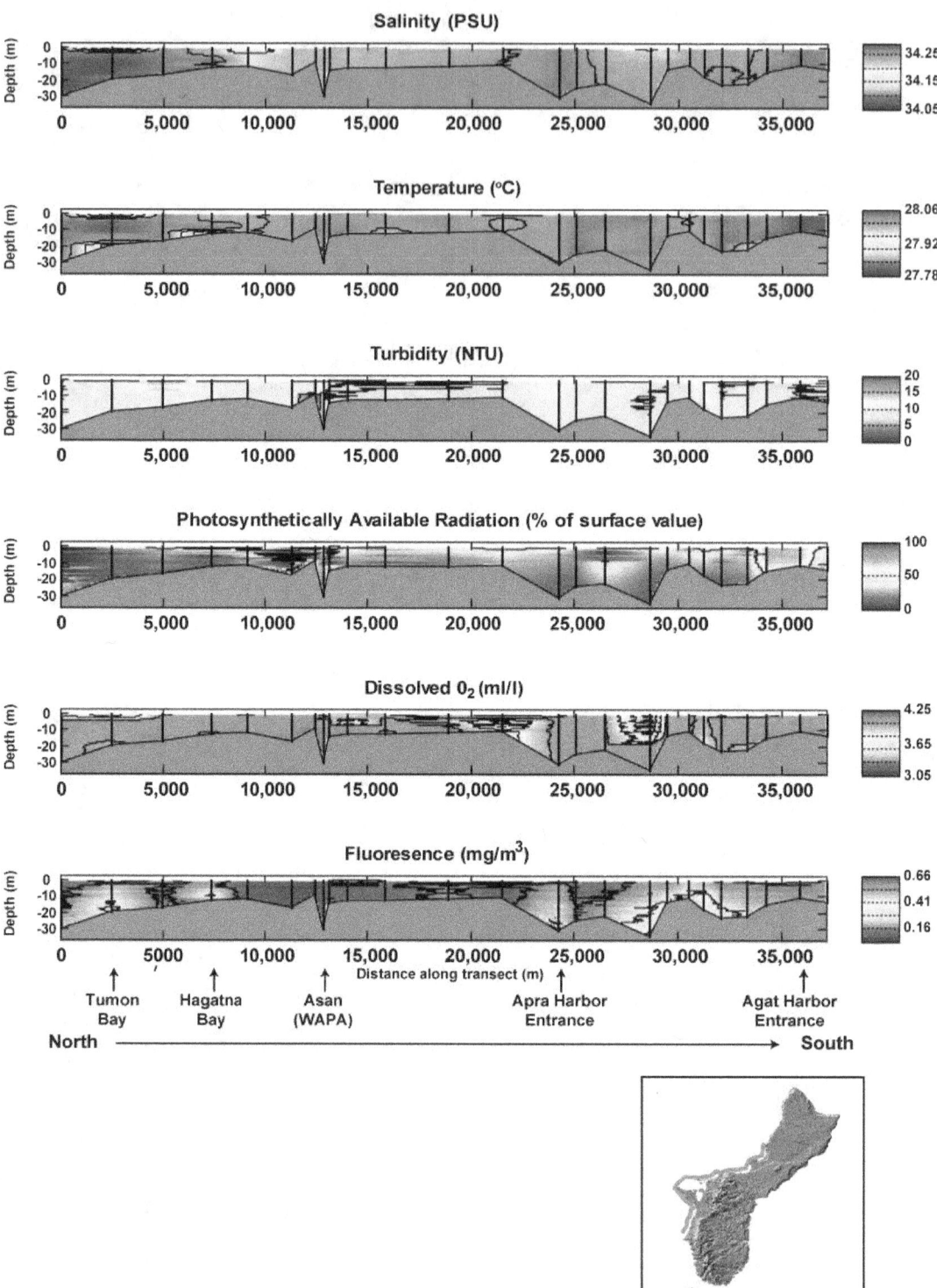

**Figure 11.** Alongshore variability in water column properties off west-central Guam in January 2008. *A,* Salinity, in Practical Salinity Units. *B,* Temperature, in degrees Celsius. *C,* Turbidity, in Nephelometric Turbidity Units. *D,* Photosynthetically-available radiation, in percent of surface value. *E,* Dissolved oxygen, in milliliters per liter. *F,* Fluorescence, in milligrams per cubic meter. Note the high variability both within the water column at a given location and alongshore between sites.

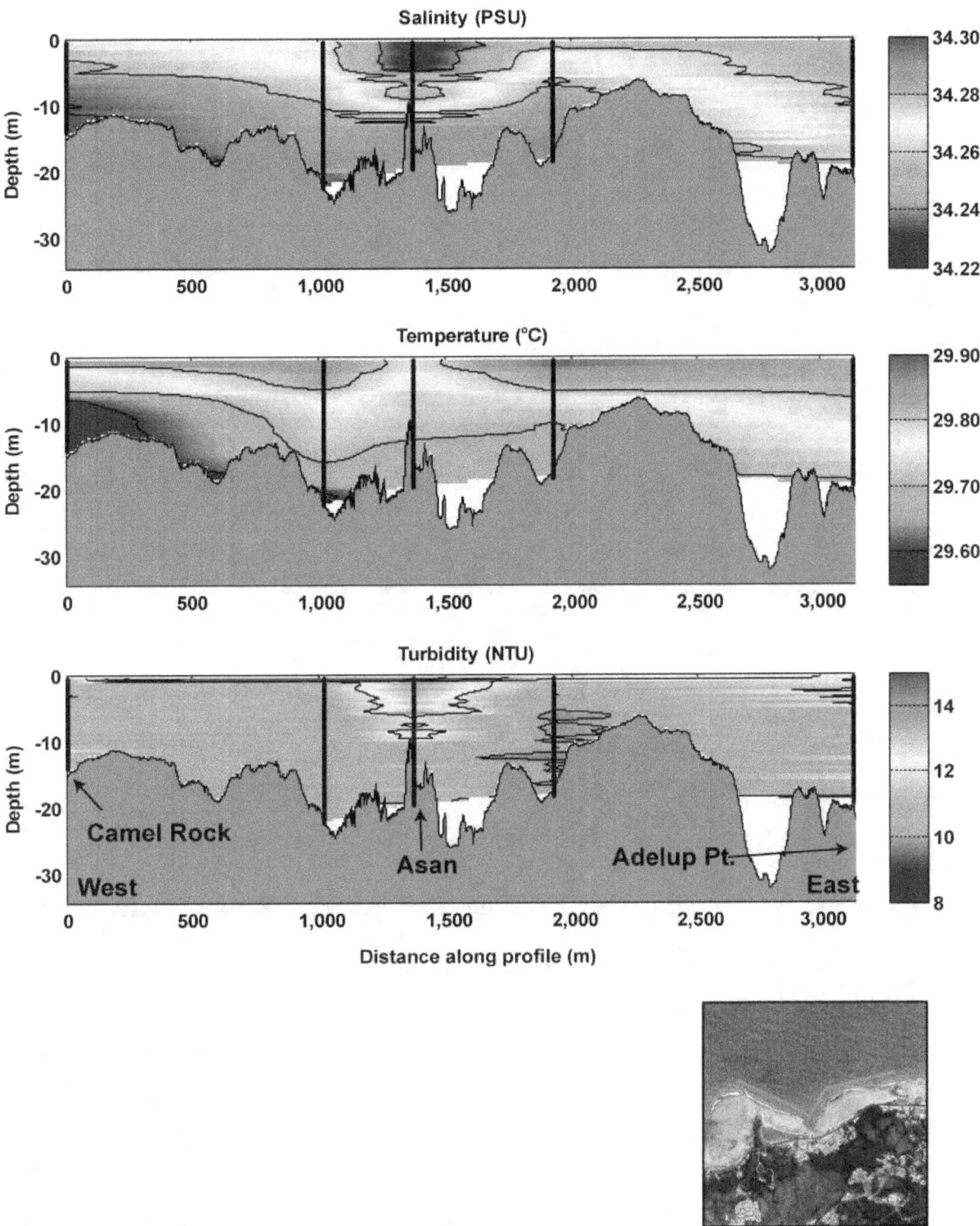

**WAPA Shore Parallel, July 23, 2007**

Salinity (PSU)

Temperature (°C)

Turbidity (NTU)

Camel Rock

Asan

Adelup Pt.

West

East

Distance along profile (m)

Figure 12. Alongshore variability in water column properties in Asan Bay in July 2007. *A,* Salinity, in Practical Salinity Units. *B,* Temperature, in degrees Celsius. *C,* Turbidity, in Nephelometric Turbidity Units. Note the lower salinity and higher turbidity at the Cut off the Asan River.

# WAPA Shore Normal, July 23, 2007

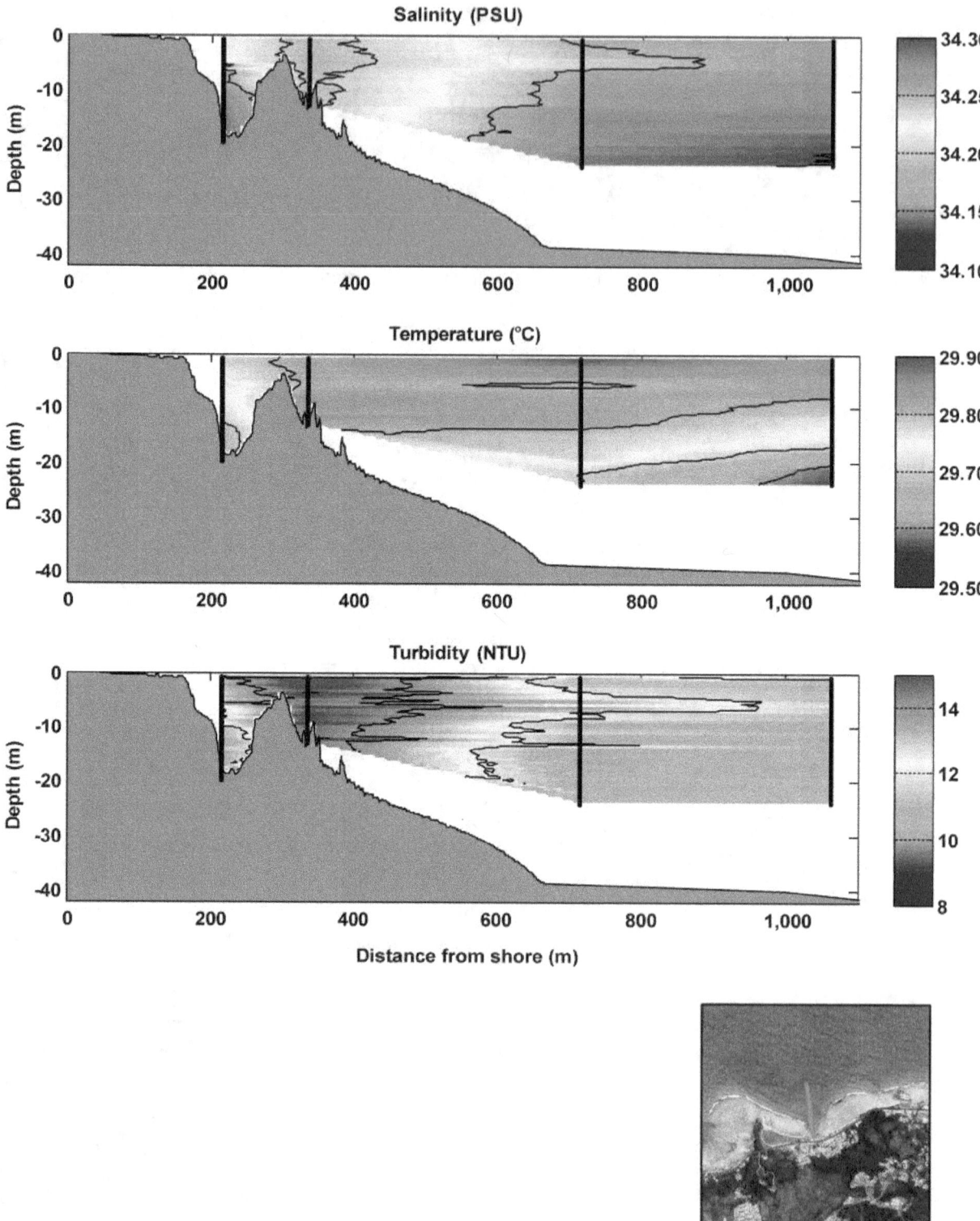

Figure 13. Cross-shore variability in water column properties in Asan Bay in July 2007. *A,* Salinity, in Practical Salinity Units. *B,* Temperature, in degrees Celsius. *C,* Turbidity, in Nephelometric Turbidity Units. Note the lower salinity and higher turbidity closer to shore off the Cut off the Asan River.

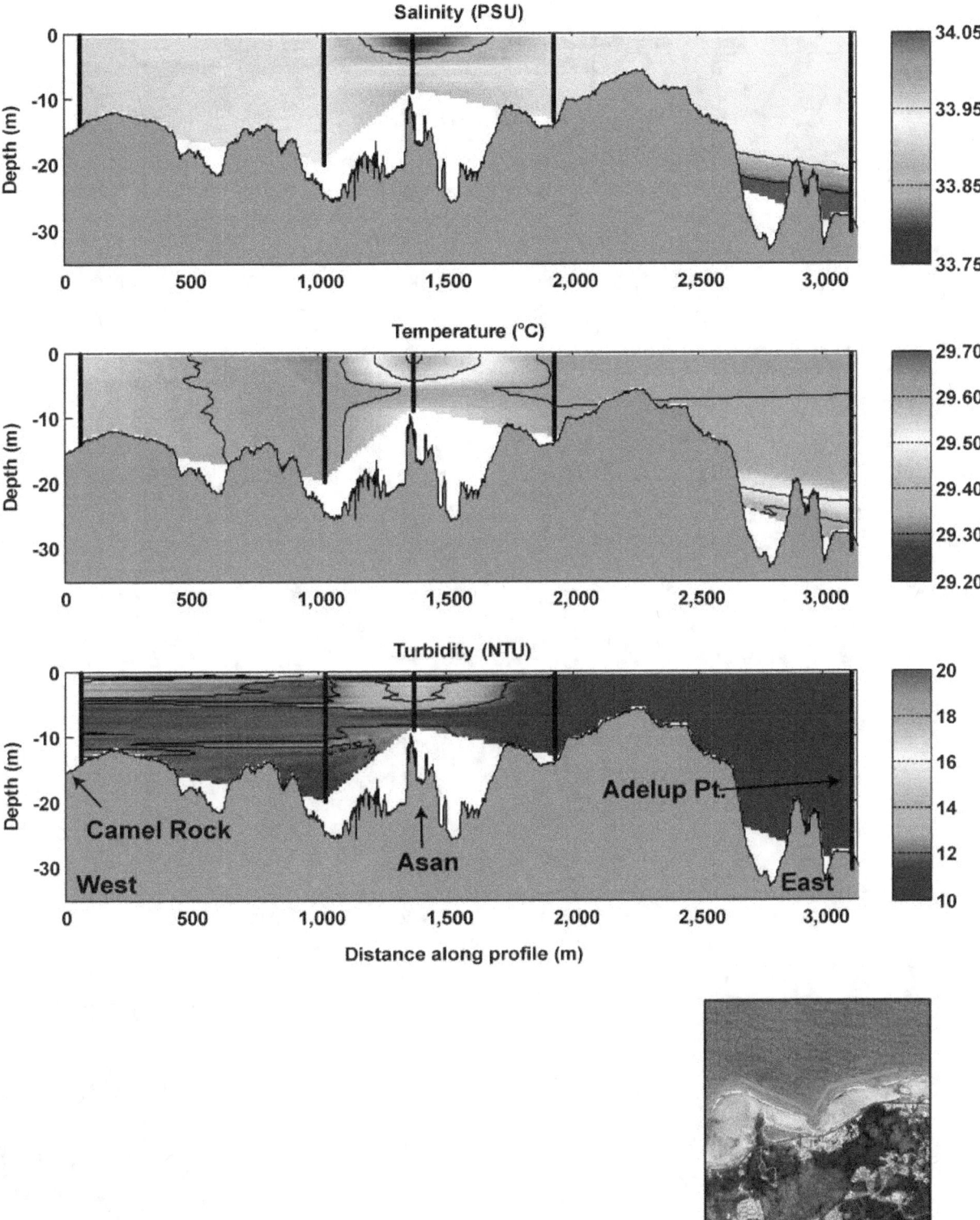

**Figure 14.** Alongshore variability in water column properties in Asan Bay in November 2007. *A,* Salinity, in Practical Salinity Units. *B,* Temperature, in degrees Celsius. *C,* Turbidity, in Nephelometric Turbidity Units. Note the lower salinity and higher turbidity at the Cut off the Asan River.

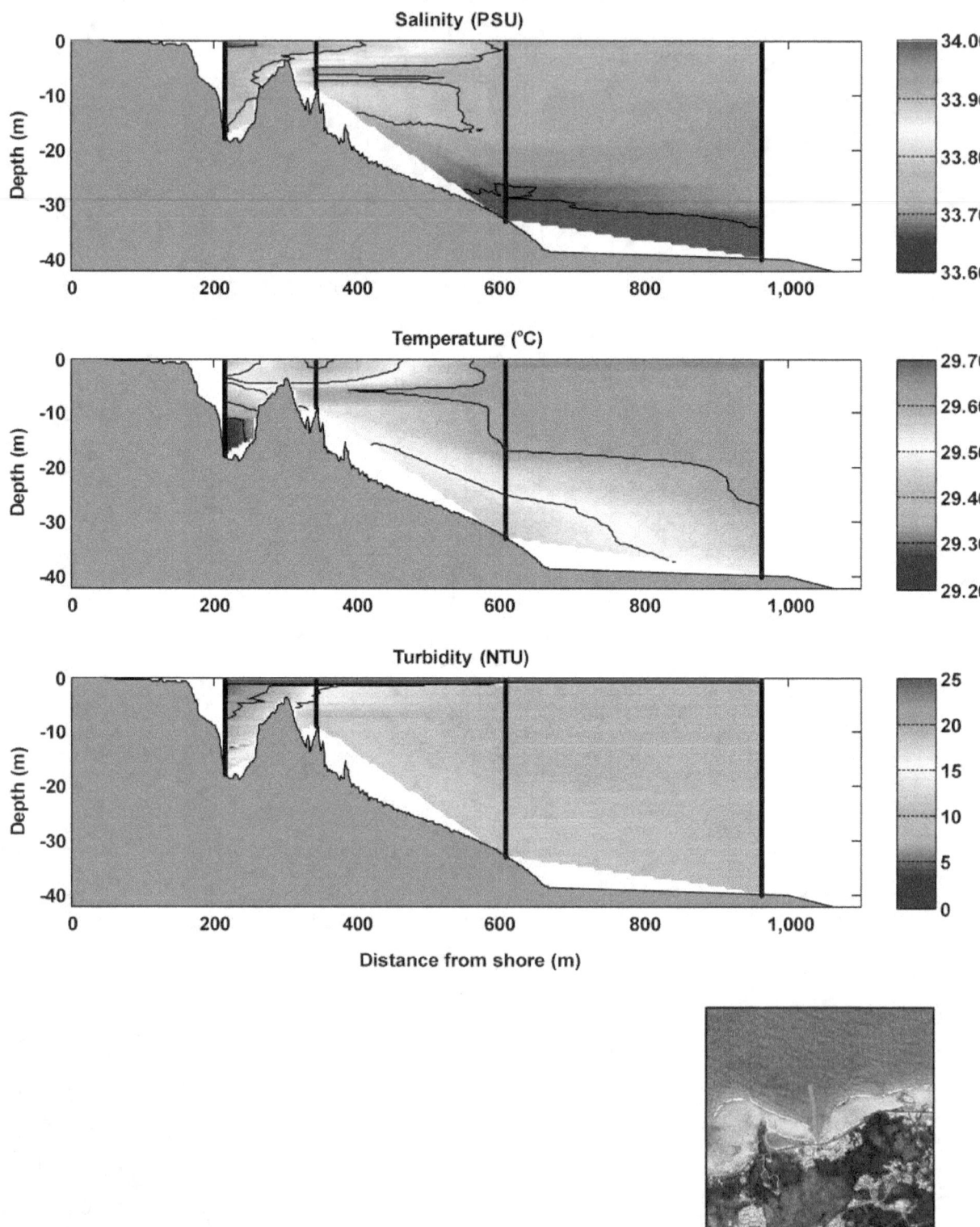

**Figure 15.** Cross-shore variability in water column properties in Asan Bay in November 2007. *A,* Salinity, in Practical Salinity Units. *B,* Temperature, in degrees Celsius. *C,* Turbidity, in Nephelometric Turbidity Units. Note the lower salinity and higher turbidity closer to shore off the Cut off the Asan River.

# WAPA Shore Parallel, February 1, 2008

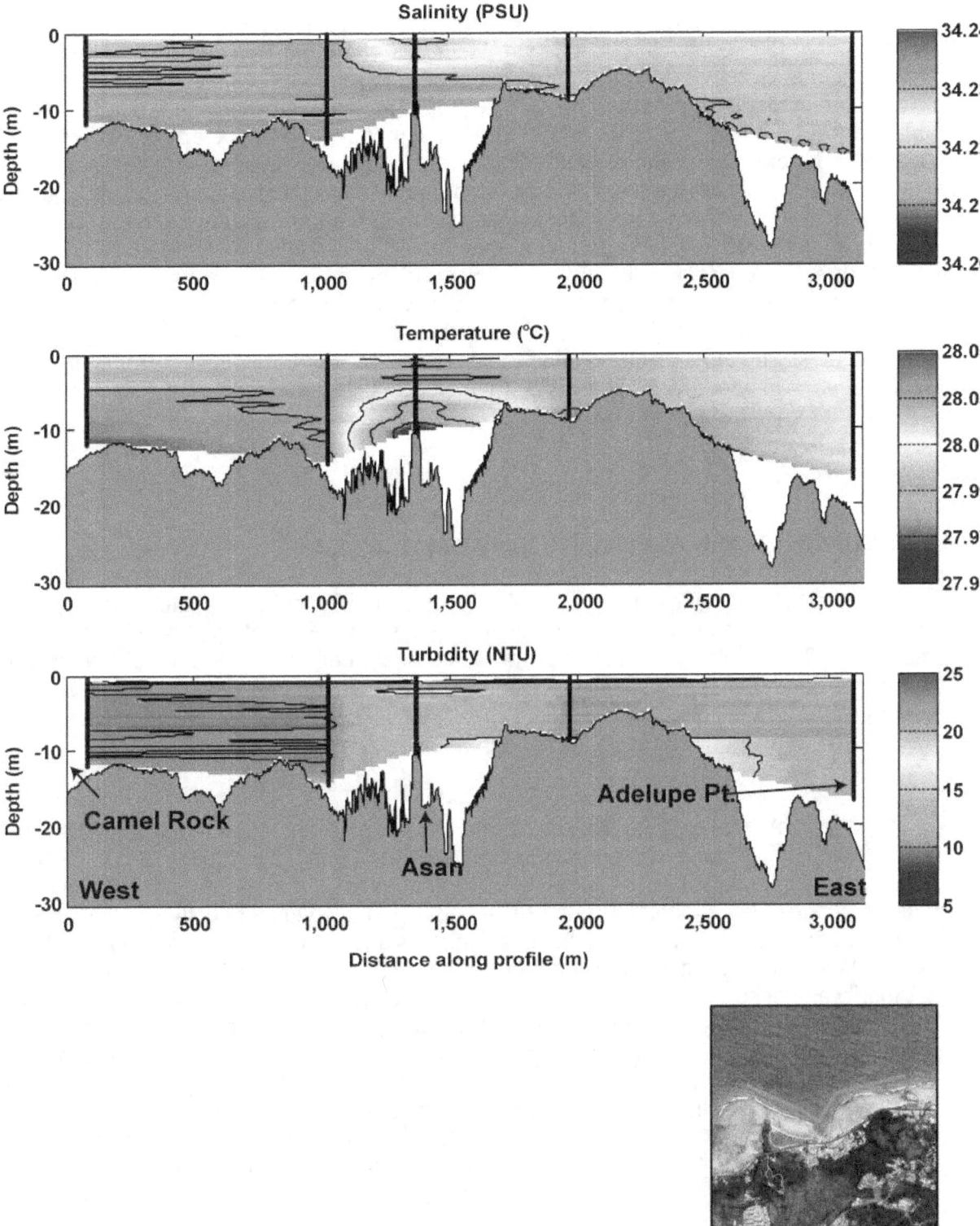

Figure 16. Alongshore variability in water column properties in Asan Bay in January 2008. *A,* Salinity, in Practical Salinity Units. *B,* Temperature, in degrees Celsius. *C,* Turbidity, in Nephelometric Turbidity Units. Note the lower salinity and higher turbidity at the Cut off the Asan River.

Cut. Similar to the model runs with the waves out of the northeast, the patterns of wave breaking from northwesterly waves drive flow shoreward across the reef crest onto the reef flat. In these model runs, however, the currents are weaker to the west along the eastern half of the reef flat and stronger to the east along the western half of the reef flat, converging primarily into the Cut and, to a much lesser extent, at a location on the reef crest approximately 200 m to the west of Adelup Point in the region where wave breaking is minimal (fig. 22b). Please note that the strong offshore-directed currents off Adelup Point in the model are an edge effect of the model and are not real. The offshore-directed return flow in the case of northwesterly waves is then driven to the northeast and east upon exiting the Cut, primarily due to wave-driven flow over the fore reef. Similar to the model runs with northeasterly waves, the difference between the wave breaking and flow patterns due to larger storm waves (fig. 22) and smaller wind waves (fig. 23) is in the greater fraction of breaking at the reef crest, resulting in faster current speeds on the reef flat during the larger storm waves than during trade wind-wave forcing. In all model runs, the Cut appears to be a conduit for the reef to shed water driven up onto the reef flat by wind- and wave-driven flows, with the final direction of the water exiting the Cut being controlled by the orientation of incident wind- and wave-driven forcing.

# Discussion

## Spatial and Temporal Variability in Circulation Patterns

Tides, trade winds, and waves all occurred on different time scales during the experiment and contributed to the overall circulation in the bay and the resulting flux of freshwater and sediment. The resulting circulation patterns are described below for each of the oceanographic conditions and their implications for the delivery of sediment to areas of active coral growth and benthic habitats.

Tides

Most of the daily variability in current speed and direction at the study sites was due to the tides. The magnitude of the tidal currents is driven by the lunar tidal cycle, with the highest tidal current speeds occurring during the spring tides (new and full moons) and the weakest during the neap tides (quarter moons). The principal axes of tidal flow during the experiment were oriented roughly parallel to the local isobaths and showed no asymmetry (fig. 24). Mean current direction during flood (rising) tides at the 4 MiniProbe sites along the 20 m isobath was primarily alongshore to the west. The mean current direction during ebb (falling) tides at the same depth was more variable between sites, but primarily alongshore to the east. Flow under both ebb and flood tidal conditions was offshore in the Cut, suggesting that the Cut is a location of offshore return flow balancing onshore flow at other locations across the fringing reef's crest. The different flow orientations between those near the surface and those close to the bed suggest (1) some influence of bathymetric steering, possibly with the embayment at the Cut causing a small-scale eddy to form in the Cut, or (2) the volume of water draining off the reef flat influences the general alongshore flow and causes a local reversal in the shallow waters of Asan Bay.

## WAPA Shore Normal, February 1, 2008

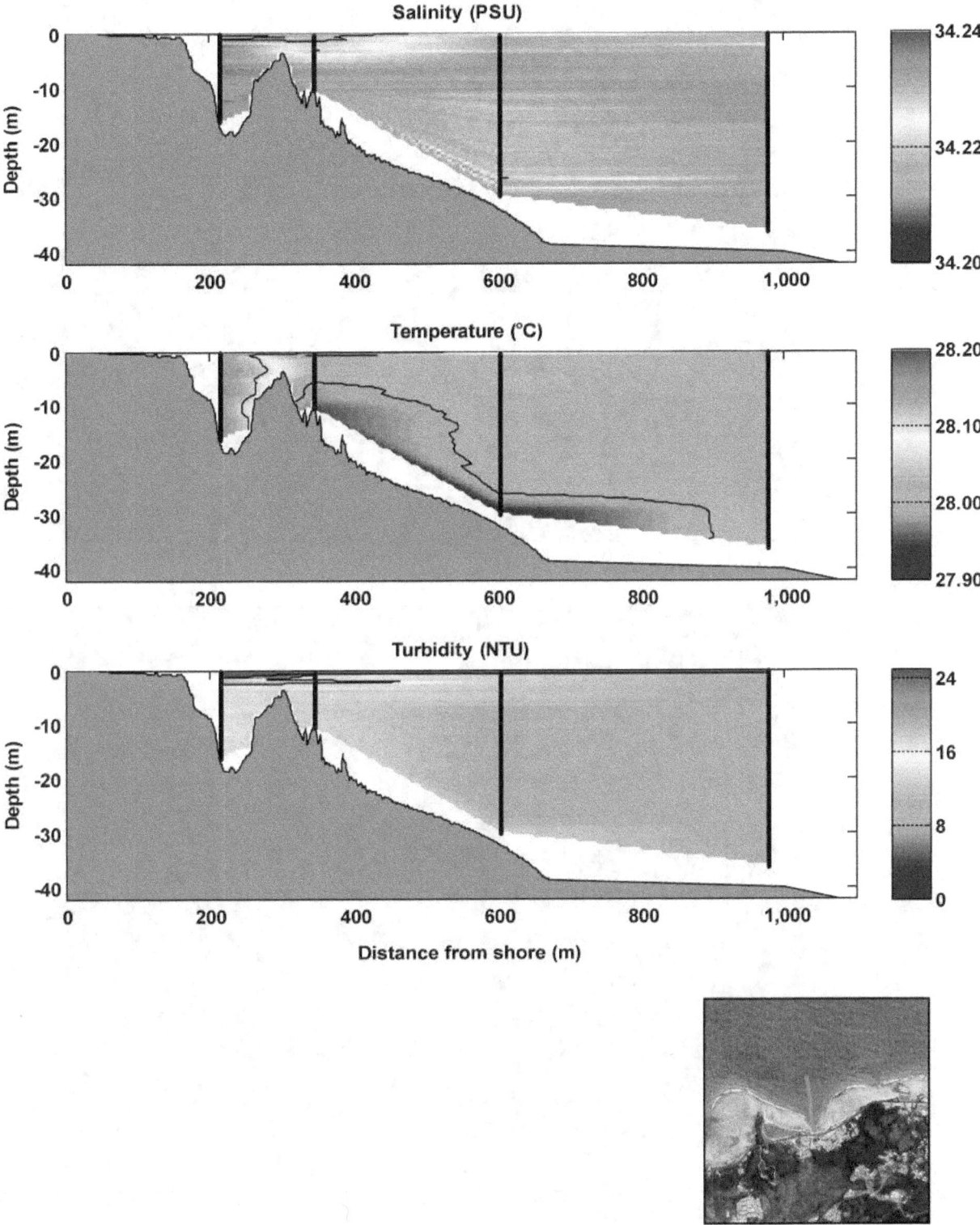

Figure 17. Cross-shore variability in water column properties in Asan Bay in January 2008. *A,* Salinity, in Practical Salinity Units. *B,* Temperature, in degrees Celsius. *C,* Turbidity, in Nephelometric Turbidity Units. Note the lower salinity and higher turbidity closer to shore off the Cut off the Asan River.

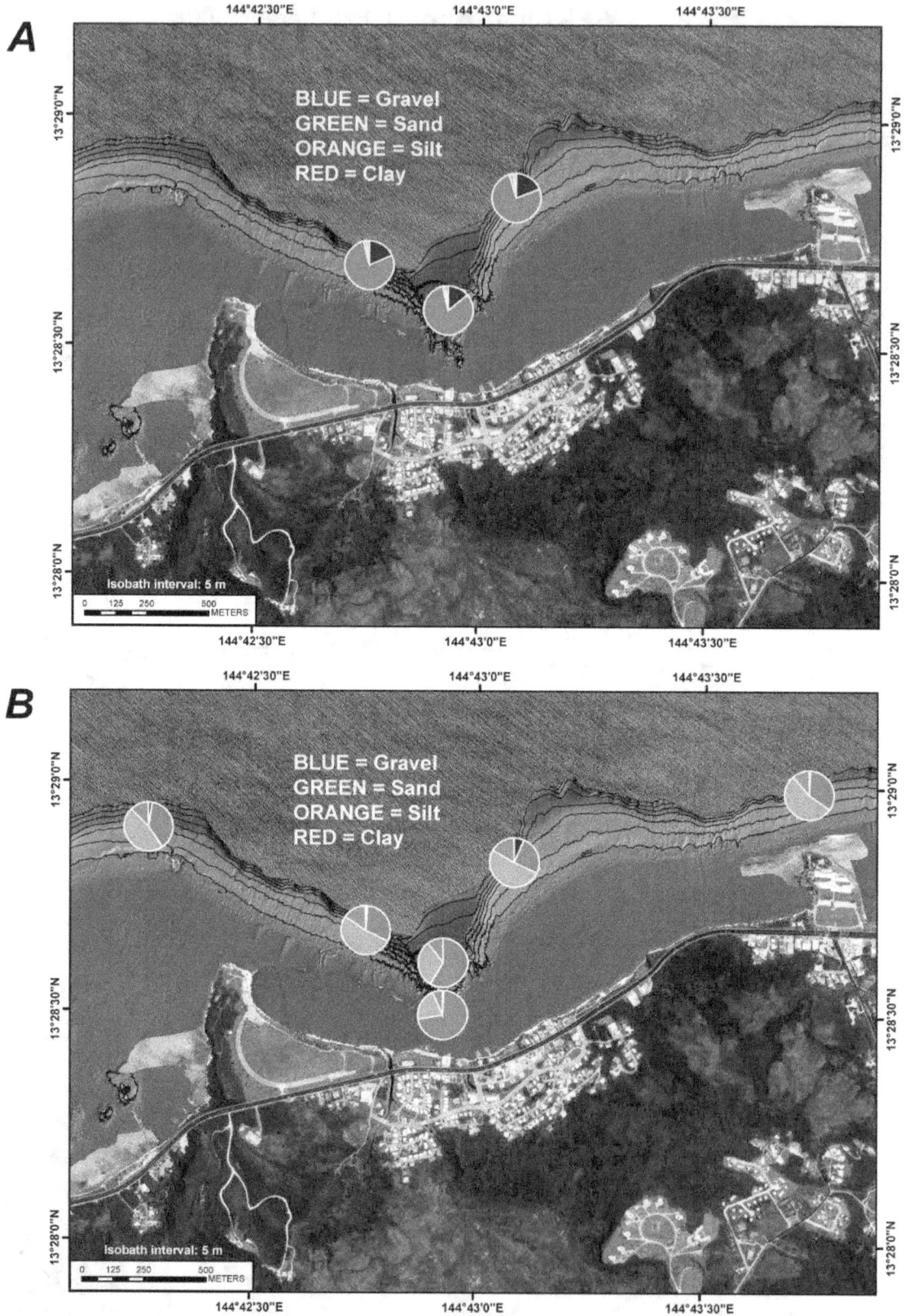

Figure 18. Grain size of sediment at the main study sites, in percent by class. *A,* On the seabed. *B,* Collected in sediment traps. The seabed sediment is coarser than the material collected in the sediment traps, except at the head of the Cut, which is likely due to material cascading down from the adjacent reef flat.

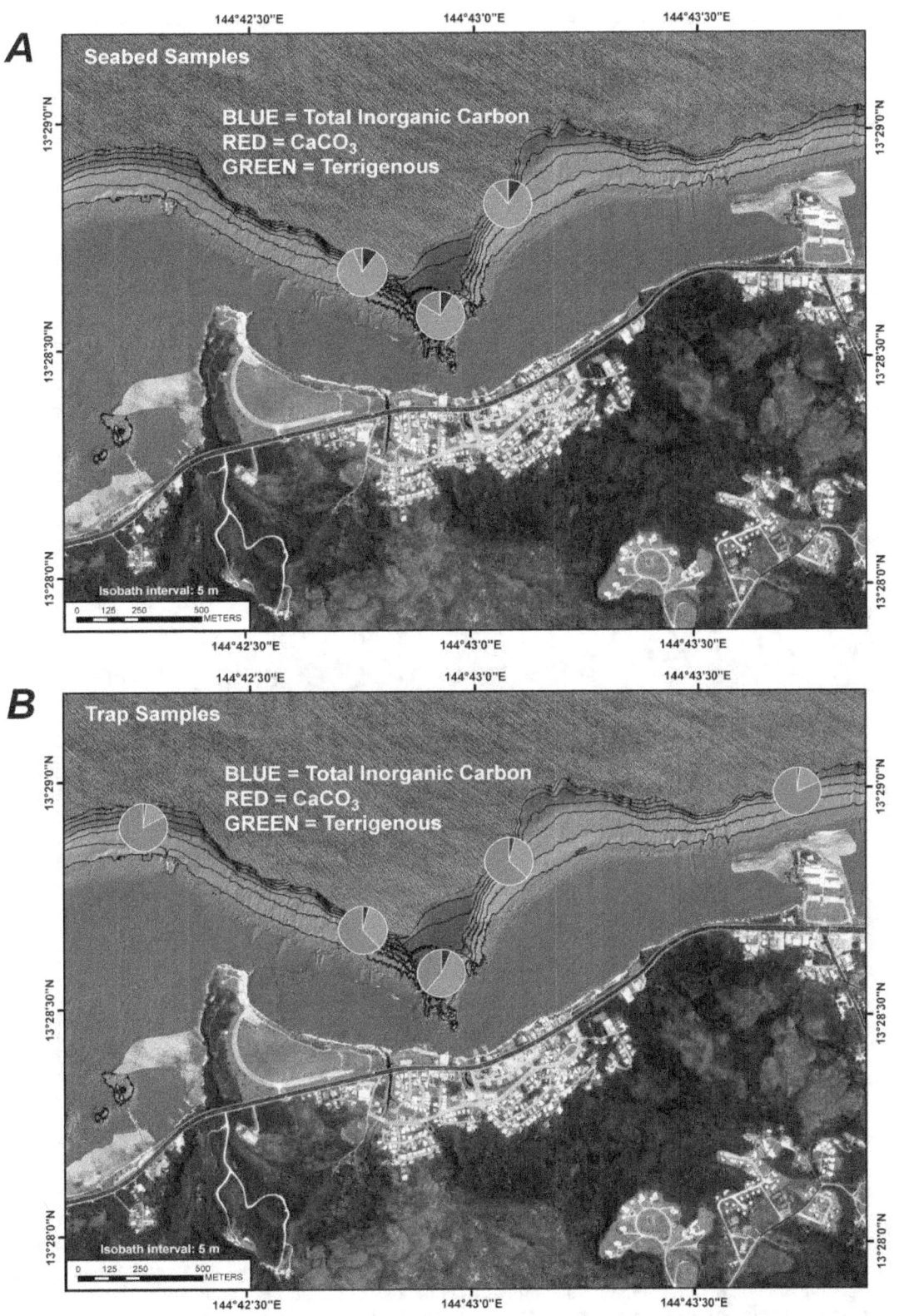

Figure 19. Composition of sediment at the main study sites, in percent. A, On the seabed. B, Collected in sediment traps. The seabed sediment is predominantly carbonate and derived from the reef, while the material collected in the sediment traps is predominantly terrestrial in orgin. The only exception is at the head of the Cut, which is predominantly carbonate and likely derived from reef material cascading down from the adjacent reef flat.

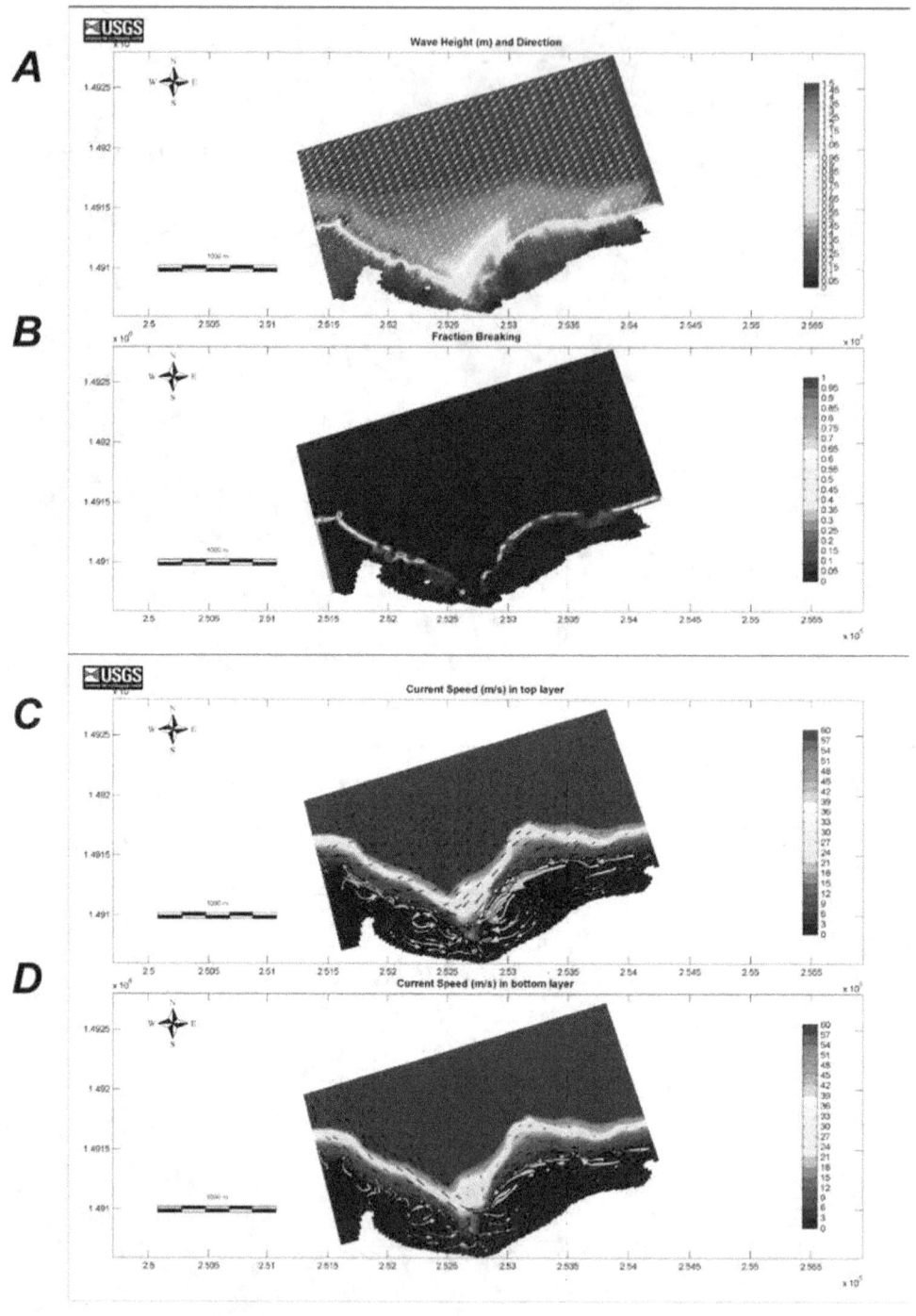

Figure 20. Waves and currents over two hours time for Delft3D modeling run w08. *A,* Significant wave height and direction (white vectors), in meters from degrees true north; significant wave height (color bar), in meters. *B,* Fraction of breaking waves. *C,* Current magnitude and direction close to the surface (white vectors), in meters per second from degrees true north; water depth (color bar), in meters. *D,* Current magnitude and direction close to the seabed (white vectors), in meters per second from degrees true north; water depth (color bar), in meters. In this run, the model was forced with 1.5 m at 8 s waves from 45°, characteristic of the passage of a storm to the north. Wave breaking is concentrated on the northeast-facing sections of the reef crest. Flow over the reef flat converges into the Cut and is driven to the northwest and west upon exiting the Cut, primarily due to wave-driven flow over the fore reef.

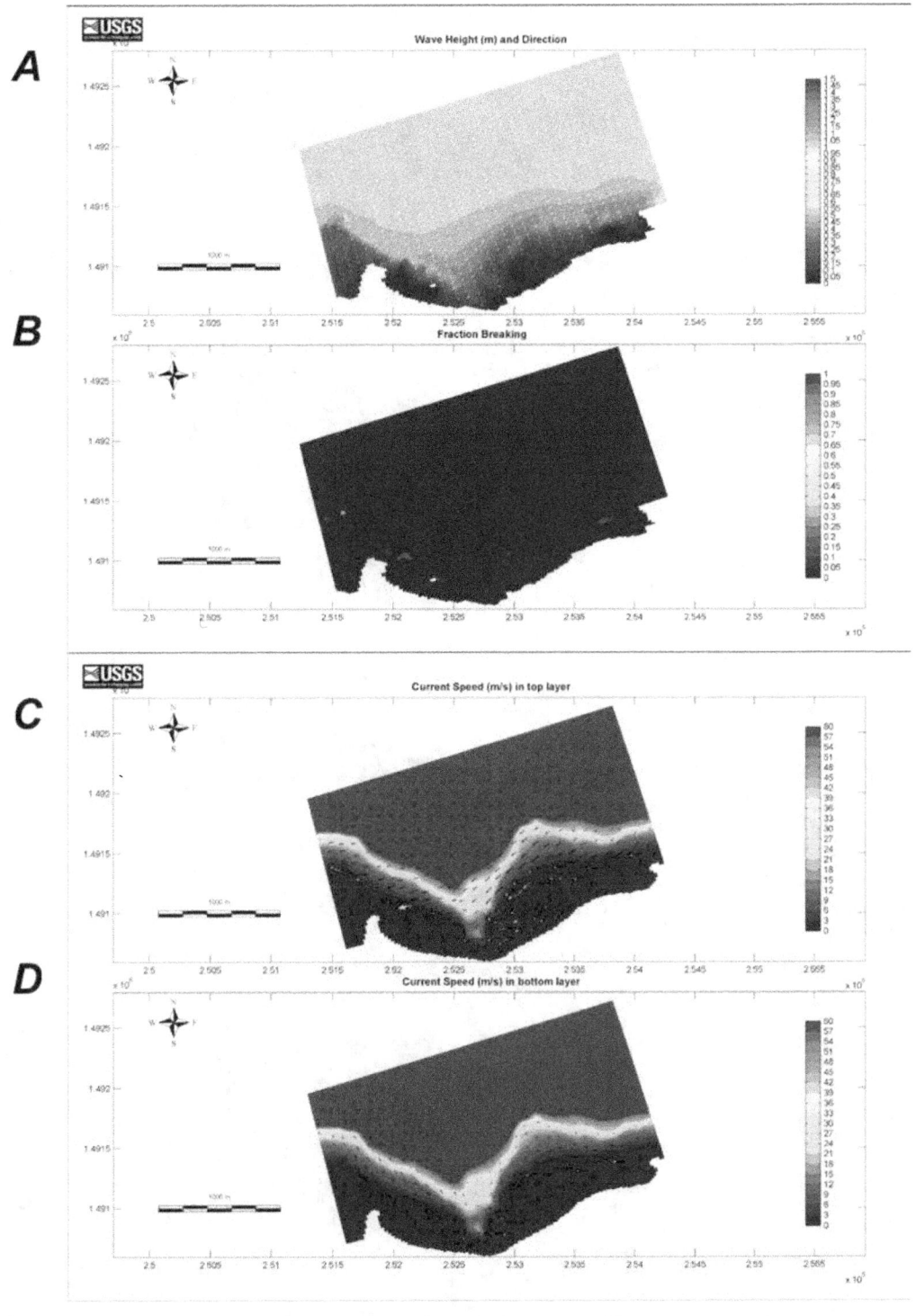

Figure 21. Waves and currents over two hours time for Delft3D modeling run w09. *A,* Significant wave height and direction (white vectors), in meters from degrees true north; significant wave height (color bar), in meters. *B,* Fraction of breaking waves. *C,* Current magnitude and direction close to the surface (white vectors), in meters per second from degrees true north; water depth (color bar), in meters. *D,* Current magnitude and direction close to the seabed (white vectors), in meters per second from degrees true north; water depth (color bar), in meters. In this run, the model was forced with 0.5 m at 5 s waves from 45°, characteristic of trade-wind conditions. Wave breaking, while smaller than that modeled in figure 20, is also concentrated on the northeast-facing sections of the reef crest. Flow over the reef flat converges into the Cut and is driven to the northwest and west upon exiting the Cut.

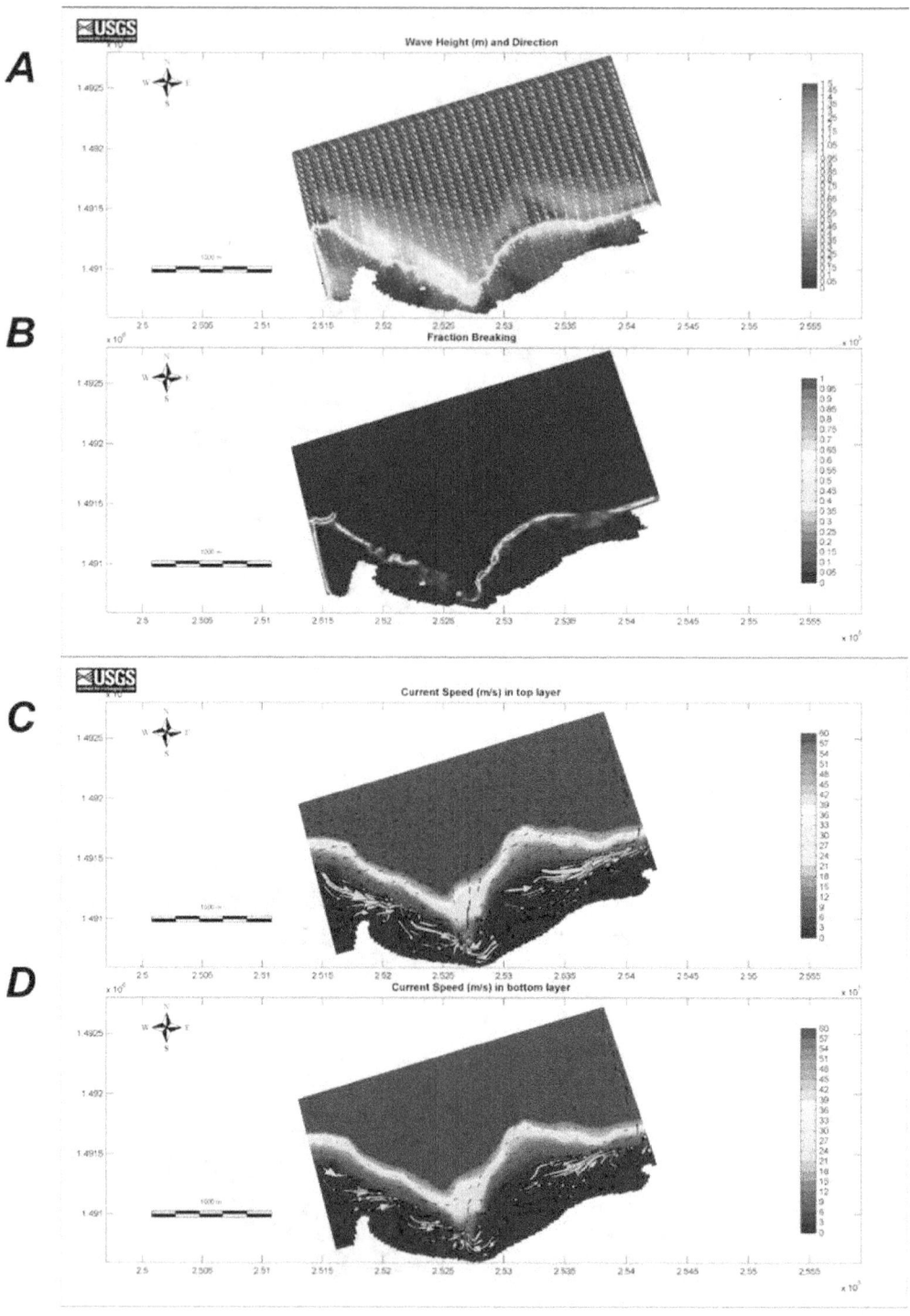

Figure 22. Waves and currents over two hours time for Delft3D modeling run w10. *A,* Significant wave height and direction (white vectors), in meters from degrees true north; significant wave height (color bar), in meters. *B,* Fraction of breaking waves. *C,* Current magnitude and direction close to the surface (white vectors), in meters per second from degrees true north; water depth (color bar), in meters. *D,* Current magnitude and direction close to the seabed (white vectors), in meters per second from degrees true north; water depth (color bar), in meters. In this run, the model was forced with 1.5 m at 8 s waves from 315°, characteristic of the passage of a storm to the west. Wave breaking is concentrated on the northwest-facing sections of the reef crest. Flow over the reef flat converges into the Cut and is driven to the northeast and east upon exiting the Cut, primarily due to wave-driven flow over the fore reef.

## Winds

The northeast trade winds are predominant during the winter and springs months in Guam and were observed in our data from December to end of the study period in February. The resulting wind direction measured in Asan Bay was primarily from the east, with a slight onshore component and a speed of approximately 5 m/s (fig. 4d). Outside of the bay, wind directions were primarily from the northeast with a speed of 5 m/s or faster. The resulting circulation patterns from the wind-driven currents for Asan Bay are shown in fig. 25. Near-surface current flow was alongshore to the west at a mean speed of 0.2 m/s. Assuming constant trade-wind forcing and flow remained constant alongshore, the mean alongshore current speed measured along the 20 m isobath of 0.2 m/s would result in a total replacement of water along the 2.5 km length of the study area between Camel Rock to Adelup Point in just over 34.7 hours. Seeing that oscillatory tidal flows enhance these mean flow speeds, the actual replenishment time would typically be shorter. The near bed current directions are primarily to the west, except at the Cut and Mid East MiniProbe sites where the flow direction is to the east. The trade winds generate a westward circulation pattern in the bay and a flow pattern that masks the effects of tides. The lack of consistent trade winds during the summer may be important for the setup of internal tides that were observed at the deep sites and will be discussed later in this report.

## Waves

Although Guam is in the path of many tropical storms and typhoons, excessively large storm waves were not observed during the course of this experiment. A few large wave events out of the north with significant wave height greater than 2 m and dominant wave periods greater than 10 s were observed. The resulting wave-driven near-surface circulation in Asan Bay was onshore at the Adelup Point, Mid West, and Camel Rock sites and alongshore at the Mid East and Cut sites (fig. 26), with a mean alongshore speed of 0.1 m/s. Assuming constant wave forcing and flow remained constant alongshore, the mean alongshore current speed measured along the 20 m isobath of 0.2 m/s would result in a total replacement of water along the 2.5 km length of the study area between Camel Rock to Adelup Point in just over 69.4 hours. As discussed above, seeing that oscillatory tidal flows enhance these mean flow speeds, the actual replenishment time would typically be shorter. The setup (super-elevation of sea level) from the breaking waves resulted in offshore-directed near-bed return flow. Although strong wave conditions occurred infrequently in the bay, they appear to be important for mixing surface water deeper into the water column and for flushing sediment off the shallow reef flat and into deeper areas of the bay.

## Spatial and Temporal Variability in Temperature and Salinity

The variability in salinity as a function of temperature for the shallow sites during tidal, wind, and wave conditions is shown in fig. 27. The primary trend shows a relatively stable salinity at approximately 34 PSU with temperature varying up to 4°C (28.5-32.5°C), indicating daily heating and cooling due to insolation. The 3 main forcing conditions appeared to have very little effect on the variability of the temperature and salinity at the shallow sites.

The variability in salinity as a function of temperature for the deeper (20 m) offshore sites during tidal, wind, and wave conditions is shown in fig. 28. The plots show 2 distinct patterns that reflect different forcing conditions. The first pattern shows increasing salinity with decreasing temperature that indicate the interaction of cooler, more saline deep oceanic water and is observed during tidal (green), wind (blue), and wave (red) conditions. The second pattern is of decreasing salinity with decreasing temperature that was only observed during wave conditions.

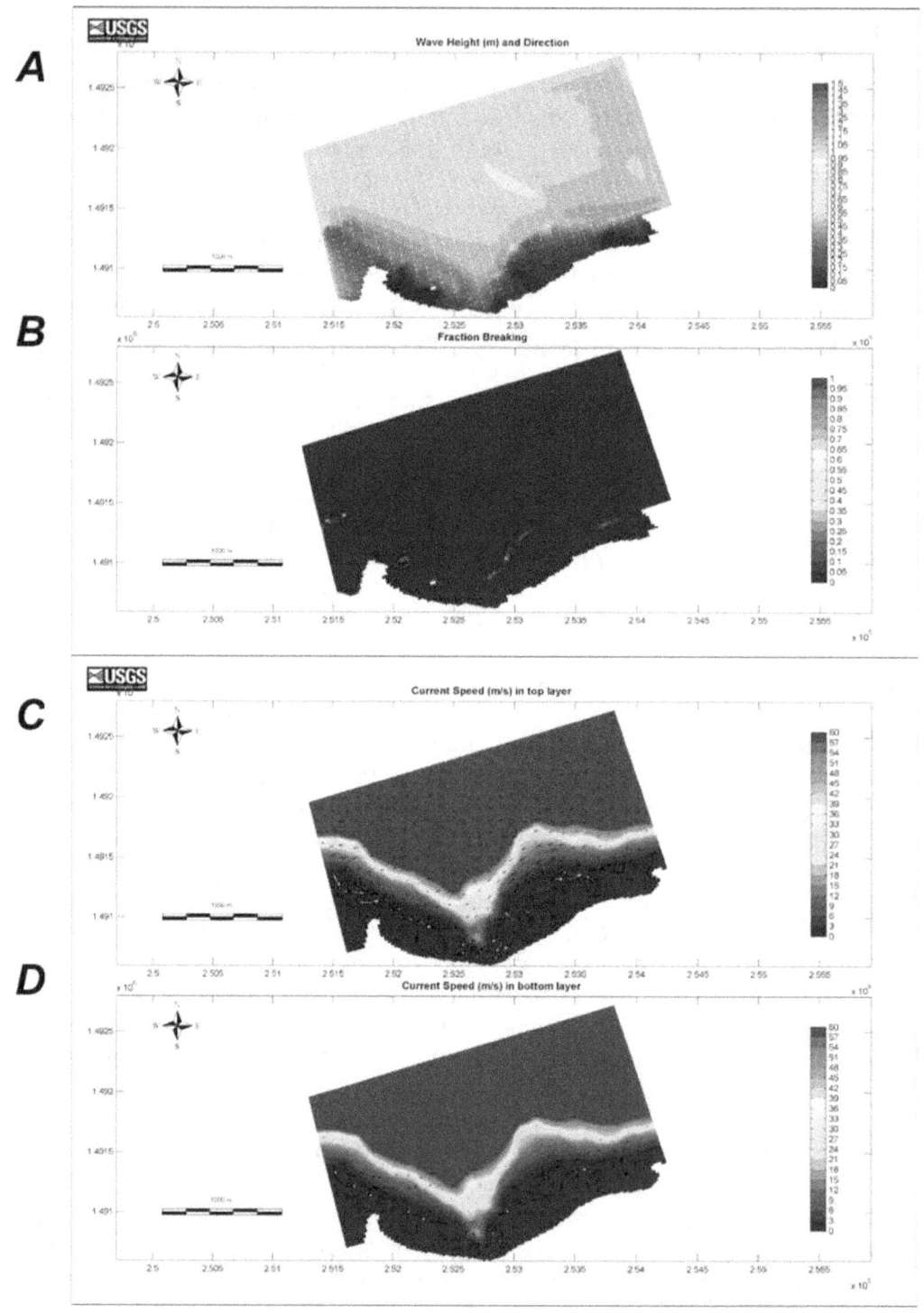

Figure 23. Waves and currents over two hours time for Delft3D modeling run w11. *A,* Significant wave height and direction (white vectors), in meters from degrees true north; significant wave height (color bar), in meters. *B,* Fraction of breaking waves. *C,* Current magnitude and direction close to the surface (white vectors), in meters per second from degrees true north; water depth (color bar), in meters. *D,* Current magnitude and direction close to the seabed (white vectors), in meters per second from degrees true north; water depth (color bar), in meters. In this run, the model was forced with 0.5 m at 5 s waves from 315°, characteristic of non-trade wind conditions. Wave breaking, while smaller than that modeled in figure 22, is also concentrated on the northwest-facing sections of the reef crest. Flow over the reef flat converges into the Cut and is driven to the northeast and east upon exiting the Cut.

This trend likely was the result of waves mixing fresher surface water deeper into the water column.  Overall, the temperature and salinity during wave conditions was lower than during conditions dominated by tide and wind forcing.

## Flood and Breaching of the River-Mouth Bar

On August 9, 2007 (YD 221), following high precipitation, the Asan River's river-mouth bar was breached at approximately 1500 ChST (fig. 4e,f). This resulted in a large flux of freshwater and sediment to the bay.  A series of photos from the TIS show the heavy precipitation followed by a plume of sediment on the reef flat (fig. 29a-d).  Prior to this precipitation event, the river-mouth bar had prevented fluvial freshwater and sediment from entering the bay. A large increase in sediment-laden (>100 mg/L) optically turbid water was measured at the Cut sites (Cut Edge, Cut West, Cut Mooring; fig. 30b-d).  The Mid West Mooring and Mid West MiniProbe sites (fig. 30e) showed an increase in turbidity following the increase at the Cut, while the other deeper sites along the 20 m isobath only showed a small increase in turbidity hours after the initial breaching of the bar (fig. 30f-h). The turbidity in the water quickly returned to near baseline values, although slightly elevated turbidity values were measured for more than a day at all the sites as the sediment was transported through the Cut and into Asan Bay.

The increase in turbidity correlated with a decrease in temperature and salinity during this time (fig. 31). A large drop in salinity (2-4 PSU) and a smaller drop in temperature (0.5°C) were observed at the Cut West and Cut Edge sites (fig. 31b,c) immediately after the breaching of the river-mouth bar due to the heavy precipitation and river discharge.  Smaller decreases in salinity (0.5 PSU) were observed a few hours later at the other shallow instrument sites (fig. 31c).  The decrease in salinity at all the shallow sites occurred for only a short time before returning to the average salinity of 34 PSU. A small drop (0.1 PSU) in salinity and temperature (0.3°C) was observed at the deep sites more than 12 hours after the freshwater influx to the bay (fig. 31d,e).

Circulation in Asan Bay during this event gives insight into the transport of sediment and freshwater (fig. 32).  The mean near-surface currents during the flood period show a strong northwest direction at the Cut MiniProbe site and variable directions at the other sites, while the near-bed currents were primarily offshore at all of the sites.  Freshwater and the initial input of fine-grained, slowly settling sediment were transported away from the Cut via the strong surface currents.  The smaller near-bed currents transported much of the coarser, quickly settling sediment discharged from the Asan River offshore through the Cut as shown in fig. 29d.

The variability of the temperature and salinity at the shallow sites shows the presence of freshwater mass as it reached the study sites. The trend of decreasing salinity and decreasing (or stable) temperature indicates the presence of freshwater. This was observed to some degree at all of the shallow nearshore sites except the Mid East Mooring site (fig. 33).  This may be a result of the dominant westward circulation pattern from the Cut and this site's location to the east of the Asan River, the largest source for freshwater in the bay. A decrease in salinity with stable temperature, although generally smaller in magnitude, was also observed at all of the deep water sites (fig. 34), indicating the freshwater mass was transported to the individual areas from the Asan River, nearby streams, and/or submarine groundwater discharge during this time period (YD 221-223). While the August 9, 2007 (YD 221) breaching of the bar was driven by terrestrial runoff and fluvial discharge, the bar could also be breached due to large wave conditions, potentially resulting in the delivery of a similar pulse of freshwater and sediment to the bay.

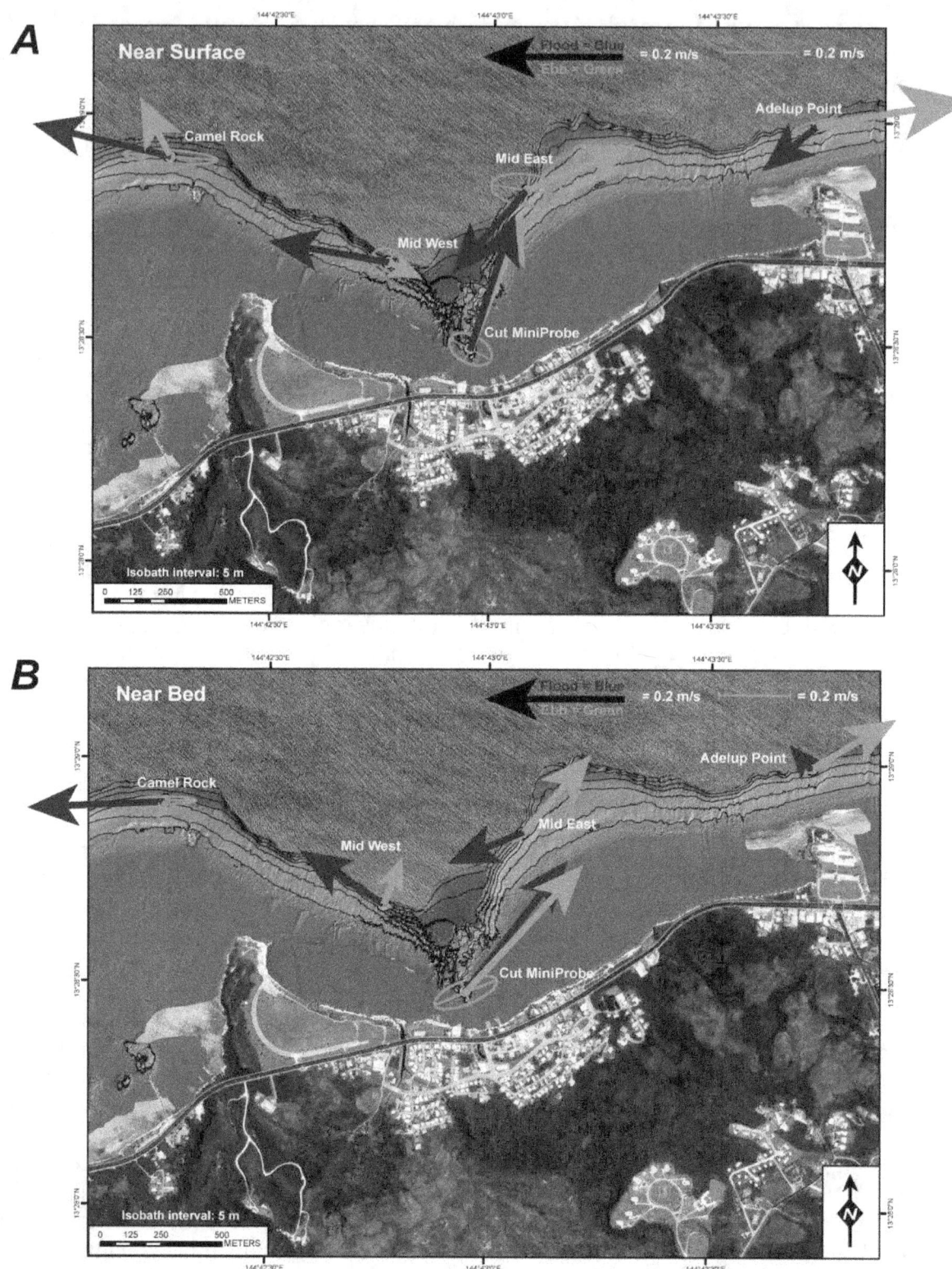

Figure 24. Principle axis ellipses and mean current speeds and directions, in meters per second from degrees true north, during conditions dominated by tidal flow at the MiniProbe sites. *A,* Close to the surface. *B,* Close to the seabed. The mean orientation and magnitude of flow during ebb (falling), and flood (rising), tides are in green and blue, respectively. The tidal ellipses (red) are oriented primarily parallel with the isobaths, with a dominant east-west direction. In general, the tidal currents flood to the west and ebb to the east.

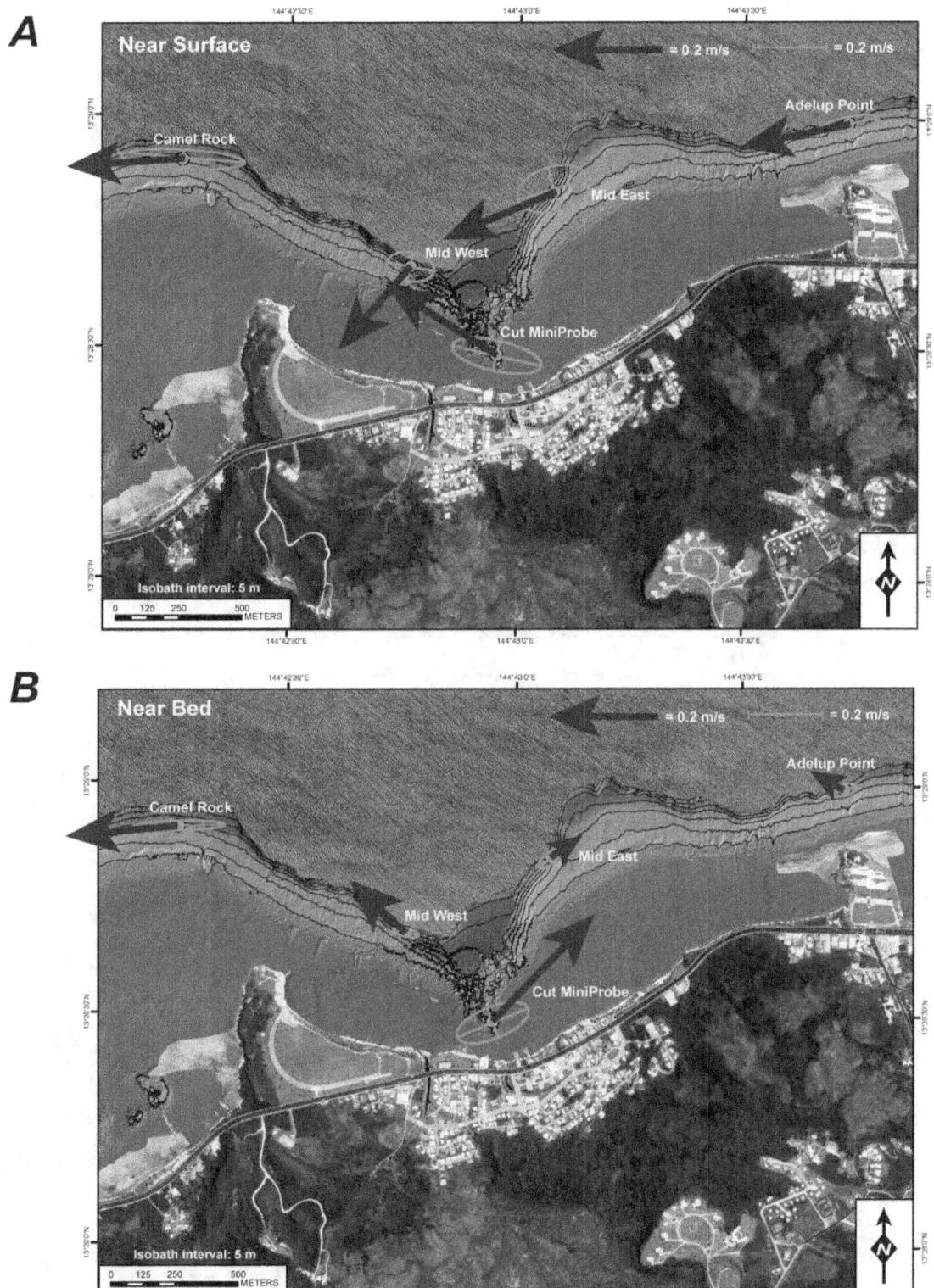

**Figure 25.** Principle axis ellipses and mean current speeds and directions, in meters per second from degrees true north, during strong trade-wind conditions at the MiniProbe sites. *A,* Close to the surface, *B,* Close to the seabed. The principle axis ellipses are oriented primarily with the isobaths and the near surface current directions are dominantly to the west in conjunction with the wind. The near bed current directions are primarily to the west, except at the Cut and Mid East MiniProbe sites where the flow direction is to the east.

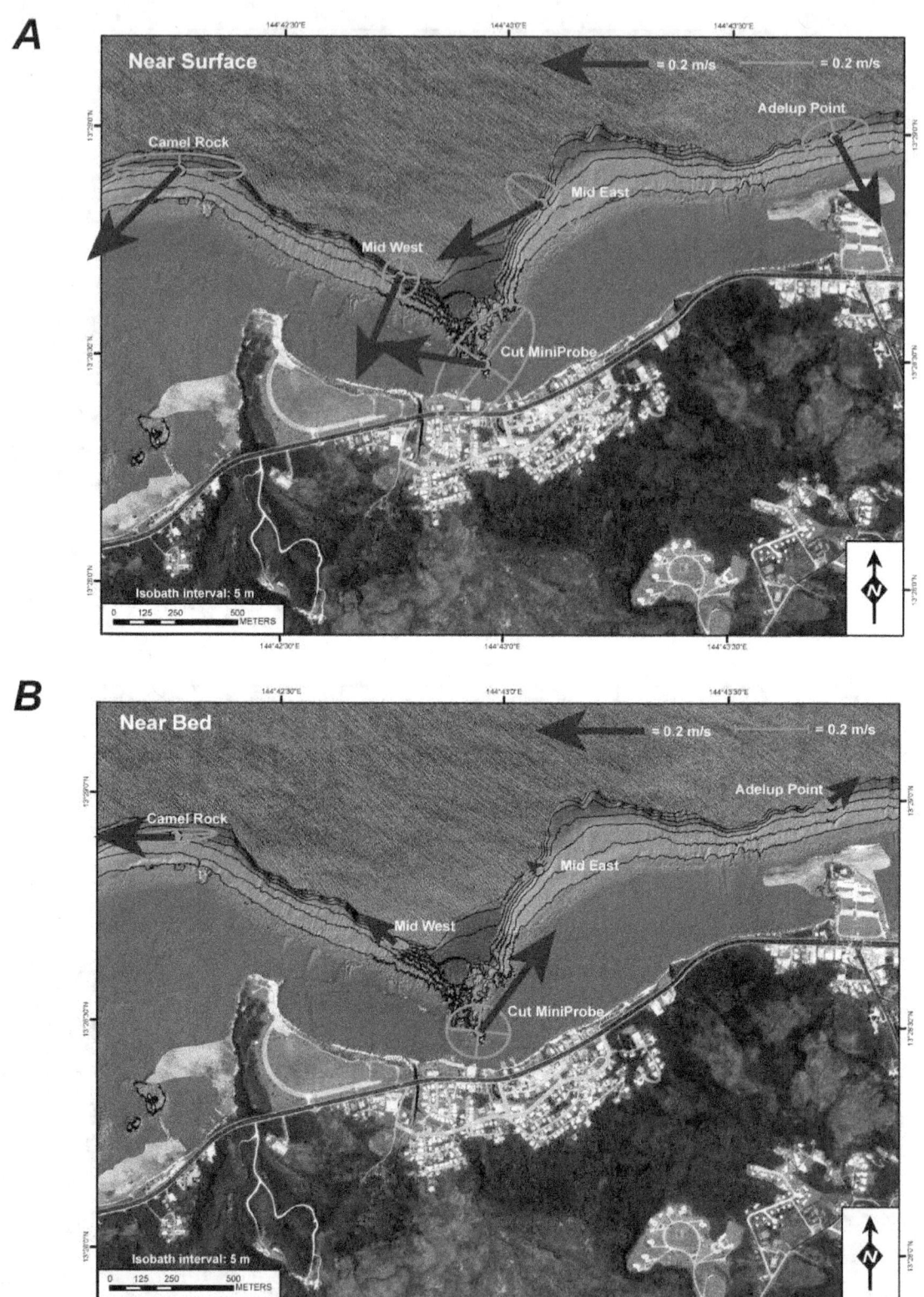

Figure 26. Principle axis ellipses and mean current speed and directions, in meters per second from degrees true north, during large wave conditions at the MiniProbe sites. *A,* Close to the surface, *B,* Close to the seabed. The principle axes are oriented more perpendicular to isobaths near the surface and parallel near the bed. The near surface current vectors show primarily an onshore direction and an offshore return flow near the bed.

42

## Circulation and Sediment Dynamics

The in situ data and numerical modeling results presented in this report suggest the following conceptual model of circulation and sediment dynamics in WAPA's Asan Bay Unit. In the absence of wind or waves, flow is to the west during flood tides, and wind- and wave-driven flow transports cool, clear, more saline oceanic water over the reef crest onto the reef flat. Return flow carries warmer, more turbid sediment-laden fresher water off the reef flat out the Cut, with a significantly smaller amount of material exiting the reef at another location on the reef crest approximately 200 m to the west of Adelup Point. This other, minor exit point closer to Adelup Point is suggested by the sediment data collected by Minton and others (2007). In general, turbidity is confined to a relatively thin, low-salinity surface layer with some settling of the sediment from the plume. Depending on the type of forcing (wind or wave) and the phase of the tidal cycle (ebbing or flooding), a sediment-laden freshwater plume will be driven either to the east or west upon exiting the Cut. Based on the grain size data from the seabed and the sediment traps, it does not appear that significant volumes of material under the meteorologic and oceangraphic conditions observed during this study are advected in any great extent to either east or west of the Cut. However, under heavier fluvial discharge and stronger winds and waves that typify typhoon conditions, much greater volumes of sediment could be transported outside of the Cut.

The Cut appears to be a conduit for the reef to shed both reef-derived carbonate material and terrigenous material. A substantial (40-85 percent) portion of the sediment collected in the traps deployed along the fringing reef was fine-grained terrestrial particles. These terrestrial particles are likely under-represented in the traps due to their slow settling velocities relative to the currents speeds and wave-orbital velocities, suggesting that while significant volumes of terrigenous sediment are likely advected through the Park's shallow waters (<30 m), these particles do not reside on the sea floor for long durations. Although this fine-grained terrestrial sediment is not observed to collect on the sea floor during the relatively benign conditions observed during this study or incorporated in large amounts into the geologic record, it is likely advected over the reefs, with the potential consequence of decreasing PAR and desorbing nutrients and/or contributing toxicants. Some researchers (for example, Marszalek, 1981) suggest that prolonged turbidity and the resulting decreased PAR are more detrimental to corals than short-term accumulation of sediment.

Based on the wave and current data collected in this study, the poor coral coverage off Camel Rock as compared to off Adelup Point appears to be due to natural wave- and current-induced shear stresses and associated sediment scour. This is reflected in the coral communities, with more delicate plate and branching successional corals observed off Adelup Point while the sea floor off Camel Rock is dominated by robust pioneering coral species. Given the typical east to west typhoon track, the western side of Asan Bay would be more susceptible to large typhoon waves wrapping around the island from the east.

## Internal Tides

The large decreases and daily variations in temperature that occurred at the deep sites during the non-trade wind period (fig. 7, YD 205-335) corresponded to relatively large increases in salinity. These coherent variations in the temperature-salinity data may be the result of deeper internal tides pumping deep, cooler, more saline oceanic water up onto the insular shelf during falling tides. An example of the changes in temperature and salinity hypothesized to result from internal tides is shown for the deep sites in fig. 35. The nonuniform temporal structure of these variations in temperature and salinity (rapid initial change and more gradual transition back to

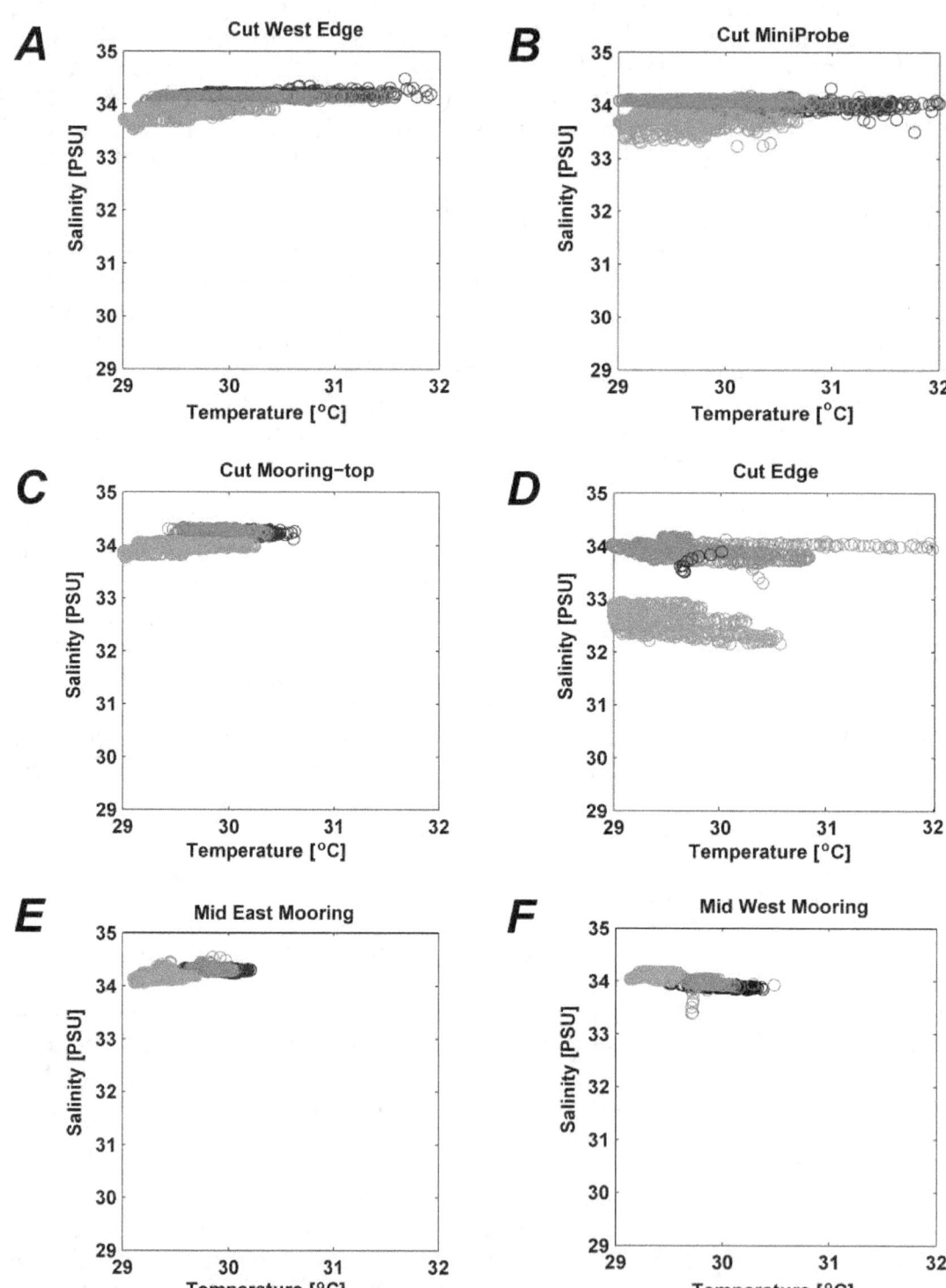

Figure 27. Variation in salinity, in Practical Salinity Units, and temperature, in degrees Celsius, at the shallow sites under tide, wind, and wave forcing. *A,* Cut West Edge; *B,* Cut MiniProbe; *C,* Cut Mooring–top; *D,* Cut Edge; *E,* Mid East Mooring; *F,* Mid West Mooring. The variation in temperature is primarily due to daily heating and cooling from insolation. The salinity signal is fairly constant for all of the conditions with slight decreases due to freshwater input.

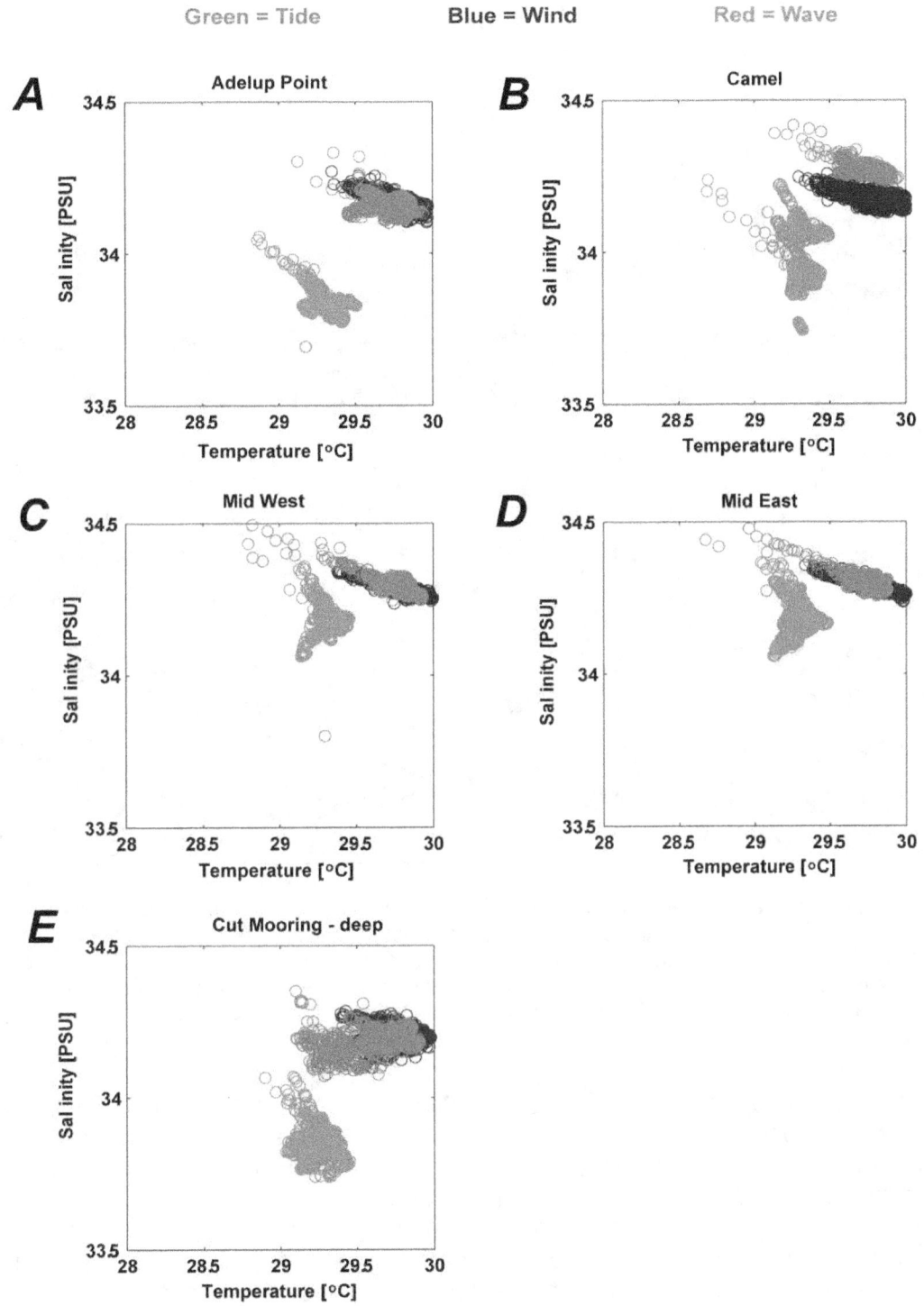

**Figure 28.** Variation in salinity, in Practical Salinity Units, and temperature, in degrees Celsius, at the deep sites under tide, wind, and wave forcing. *A,* Adelup Point; *B,* Camel Rock; *C,* Mid West; *D,* Mid East; *E,* Cut Mooring–deep. The temperature and salinity signal due to tide and wind conditions shows a similar pattern of increasing salinity with decreasing temperature. Temperature and salinity during wave conditions is marked by lower salinity and temperature potentially due to the mixing of freshwater deeper into the water column.

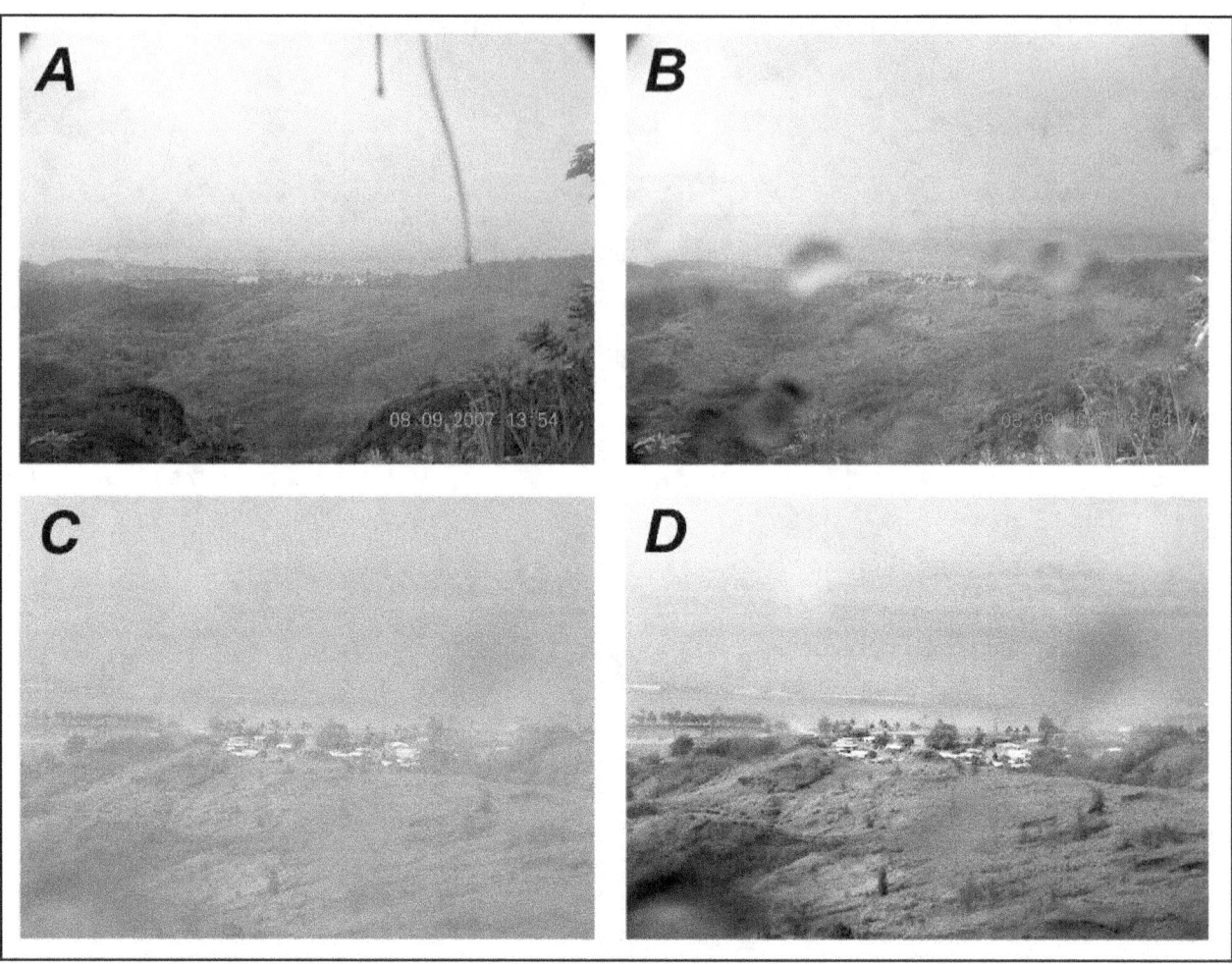

Figure 29. Images from the terrestrial imaging system (TIS) of heavy precipitation and the bar break at the mouth of Asan River on 2007 Year Day 221 (August 9, 2007). *A,* Rainfall prior to bar break. *B,* Sediment plume directly following the bar break. *C,* Zoom-in of plume in b. *D,* Zoom-in and color enhancement of plume in Part "b". The series of photos show the heavy precipitation prior to and the large terrestrial red sediment plume following the bar break.  This series is an example of the bar dynamics that controls the input of sediment into Asan Bay.

pre-event levels) suggest that these internal motions are in the form of a nonlinear bore, similar to those observed along the U.S. West Coast (Storlazzi and others, 2003) and elsewhere. A decrease in temperature and increase in salinity was observed during every falling tide during this period at the deep sites (fig. 35b,c). The change in temperature and salinity was as large as $3^{o}C$ and 1 PSU, respectively, during a 3-hour period before returning to background levels.  The greatest changes in temperature and salinity appeared to occur during large changes in tidal height, generally when the tide fell from the higher high to the lower low. These decreases in temperature and increases in salinity were not observed at the shallow sites, where the salinity generally remained constant unless there was the presence of fresh water, and the temperature generally varied only due to daily insolation (fig. 35d).

The drop in temperature occurred during times of strong vertical stratification (difference in temperature, and thus density, between the surface and near-bed waters) and reversals in current speed and direction in the alongshore, cross-shore, and vertical components of velocity (fig. 36b-d).  The falling tide generates strong alongshore currents to the east and slightly onshore

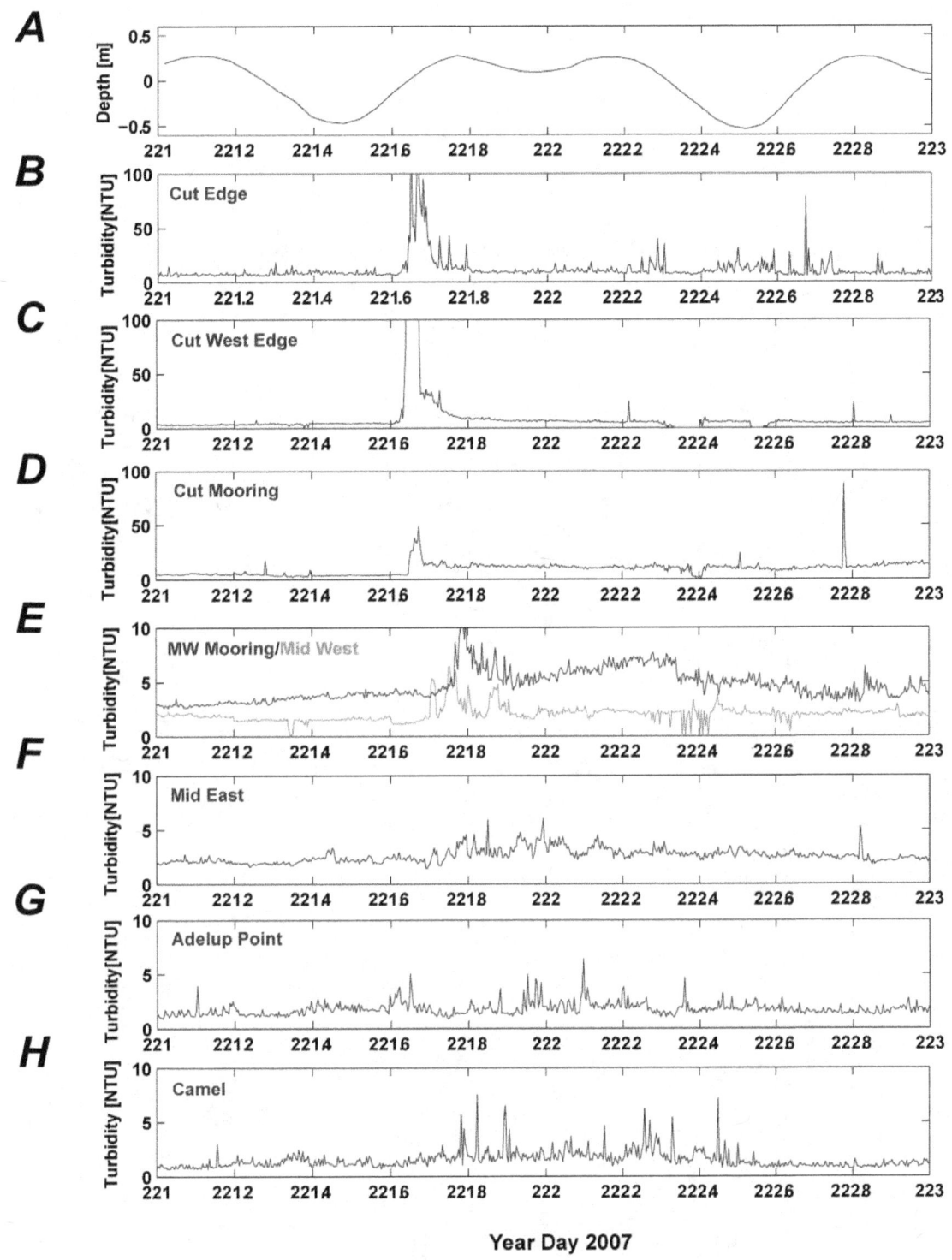

**Year Day 2007**

Figure 30. Tide and turbidity data during the large freshwater and sediment input from Asan River, 2007 Year Day 221 (August 9, 2007). *A,* Tide, in meters. *B,* Turbidity at the Cut Edge, in Nephelometric Turbidity Units. *C,* Turbidity at the Cut West Edge, in Nephelometric Turbidity Units. *D,* Turbidity at the Cut Mooring, in Nephelometric Turbidity Units. *E,* Turbidity at the Mid West Mooring and Mid West MiniProbe, in Nephelometric Turbidity Units. *F,* Turbidity at the Mid East MiniProbe, in Nephelometric Turbidity Units. *G,* Turbidity at the Adelup Point MiniProbe, in Nephelometric Turbidity Units. *H,* Turbidity at the Camel Rock MiniProbe, in Nephelometric Turbidity Units. The sites show the sediment input reaching the Cut first, then the plume moving to the west and offshore.

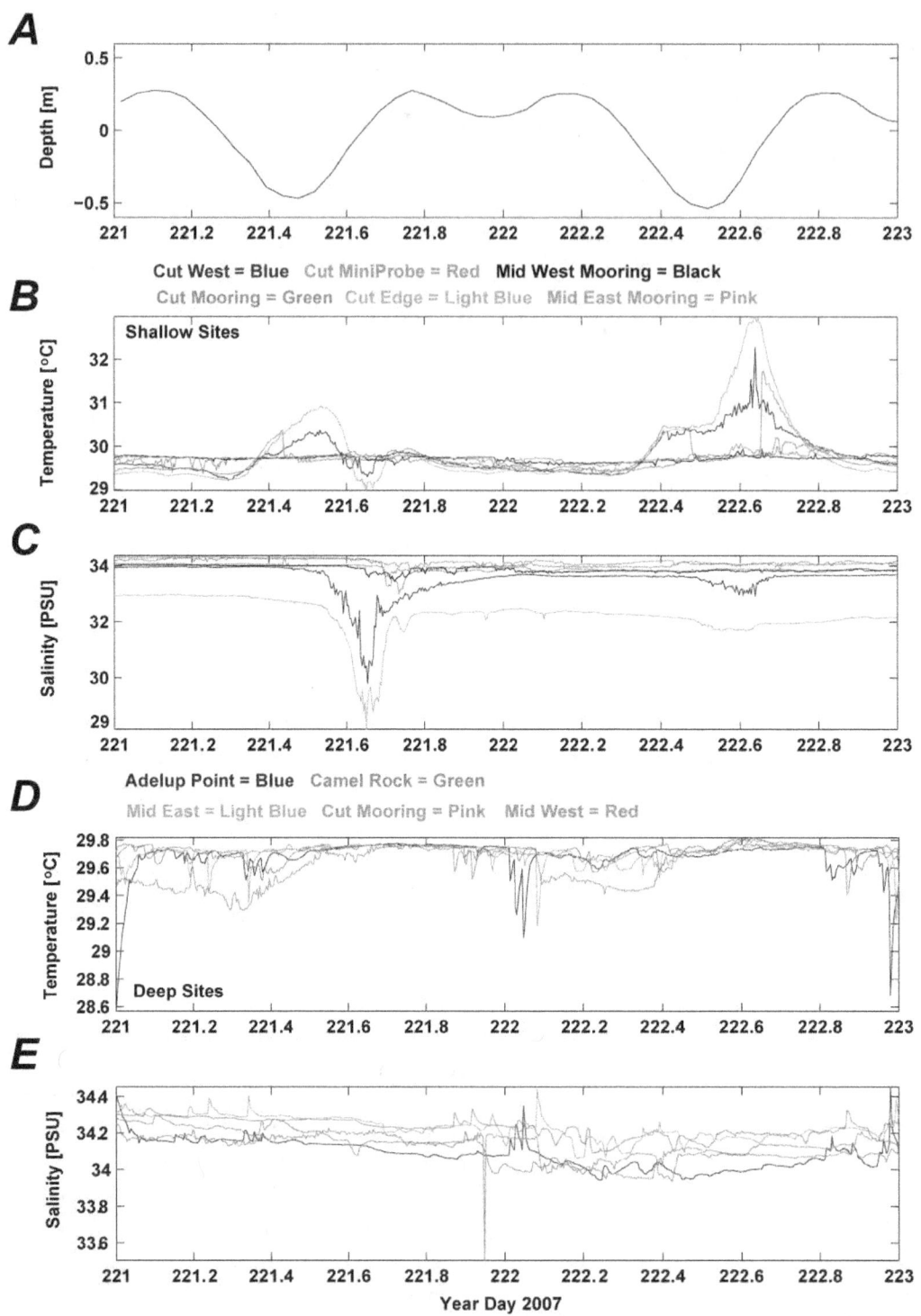

Figure 31. Tide, temperature, and salinity data for the shallow and deep sites during the freshwater and sediment input from Asan River, on 2007 Year Day 221 (August 9, 2007). *A,* Tide, in meters. *B,* Temperature at the shallow sites, in degrees Celsius. *C,* Salinity at the shallow sites, in Practical Salinity Units. *D,* Temperature at the deep sites, in degrees Celsius. *E,* Salinity at the deep sites, in Practical Salinity Units. The large drop in salinity at the shallow sites shows the input of fresh water immediately following the bar break. Salinity values slightly lower than normal were measured hours later at the deep sites, suggesting that the freshwater plume was confined relatively close to the surface.

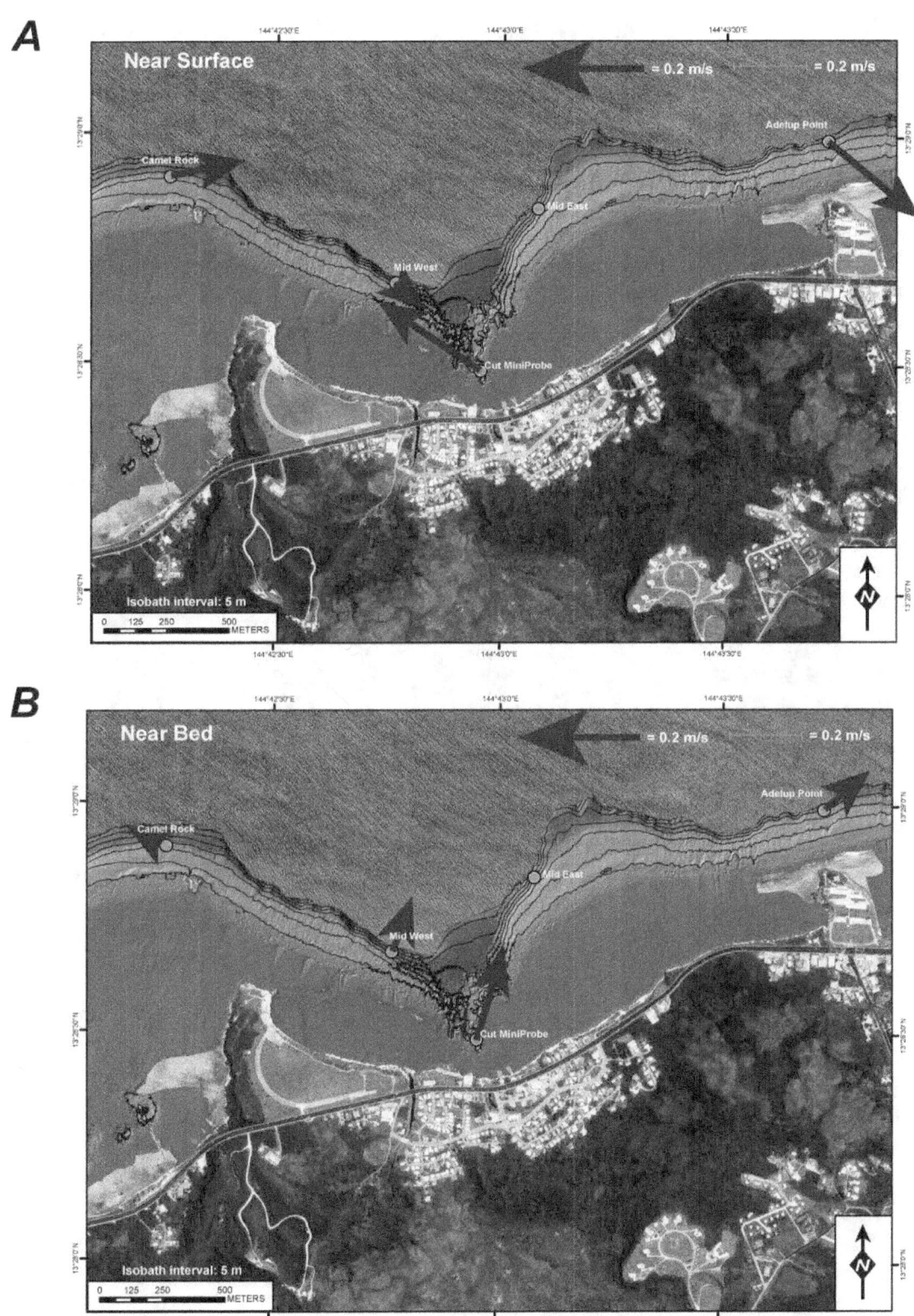

Figure 32. Mean current speed and direction, in meters per second from degrees true north, during the 2007 Year Day 221 (August 9, 2007), bar break and flood. A, Close to the surface. B, Close to the seabed. The near surface currents show strong westward flow from the Cut and eastward flow from the other sites. The near bed surface currents show predominantly offshore flow.

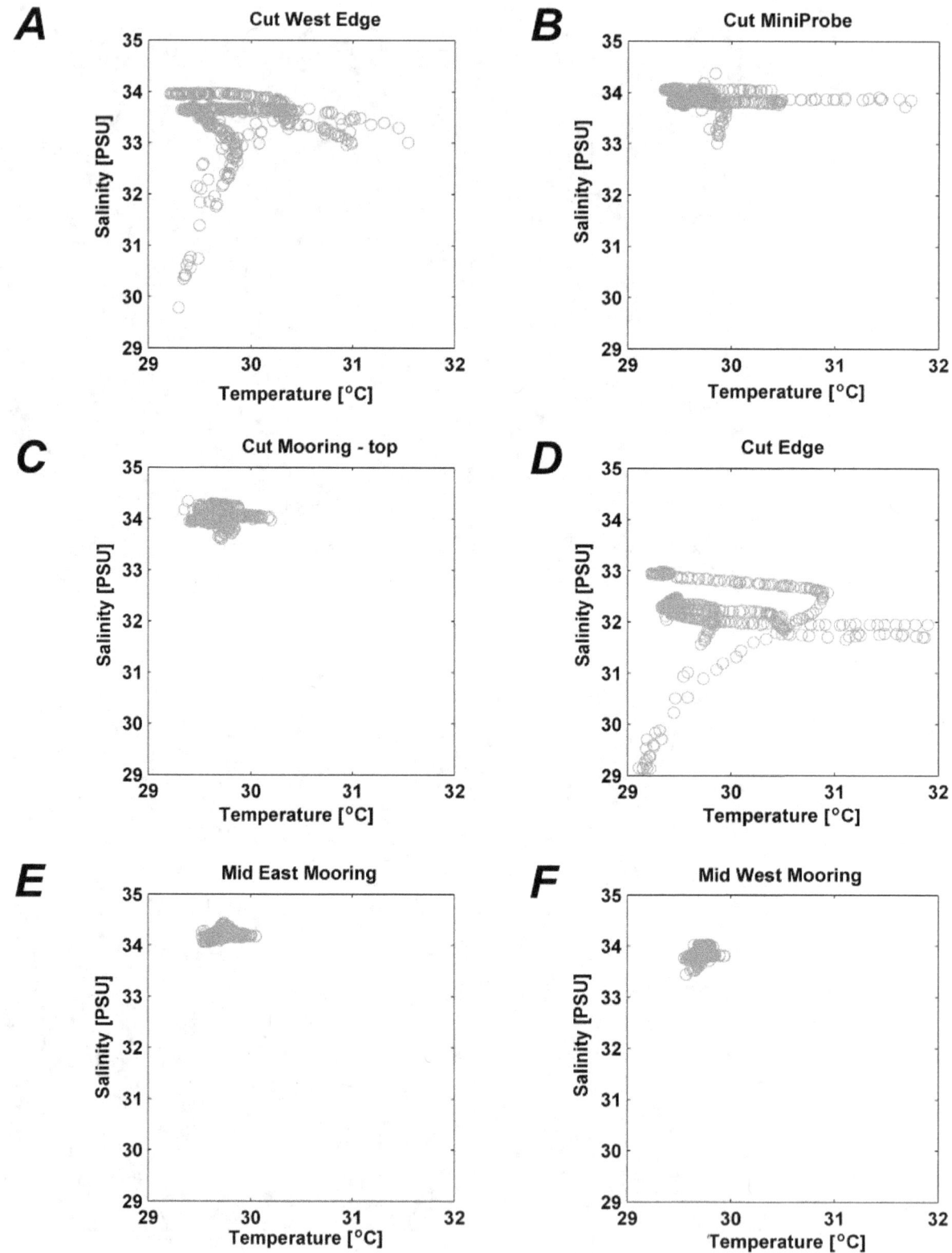

Figure 33. Variation in salinity, in Practical Salinity Units, and temperature, in degrees Celsius, at the shallow sites during the bar break and flood; A, Cut West Edge. B, Cut MiniProbe. C, Cut Mooring–top. D, Cut Edge. E, Mid East Mooring. F, Mid West Mooring. The Cut sites show a large decrease in salinity, with smaller decreases at the Mid West mooring site.

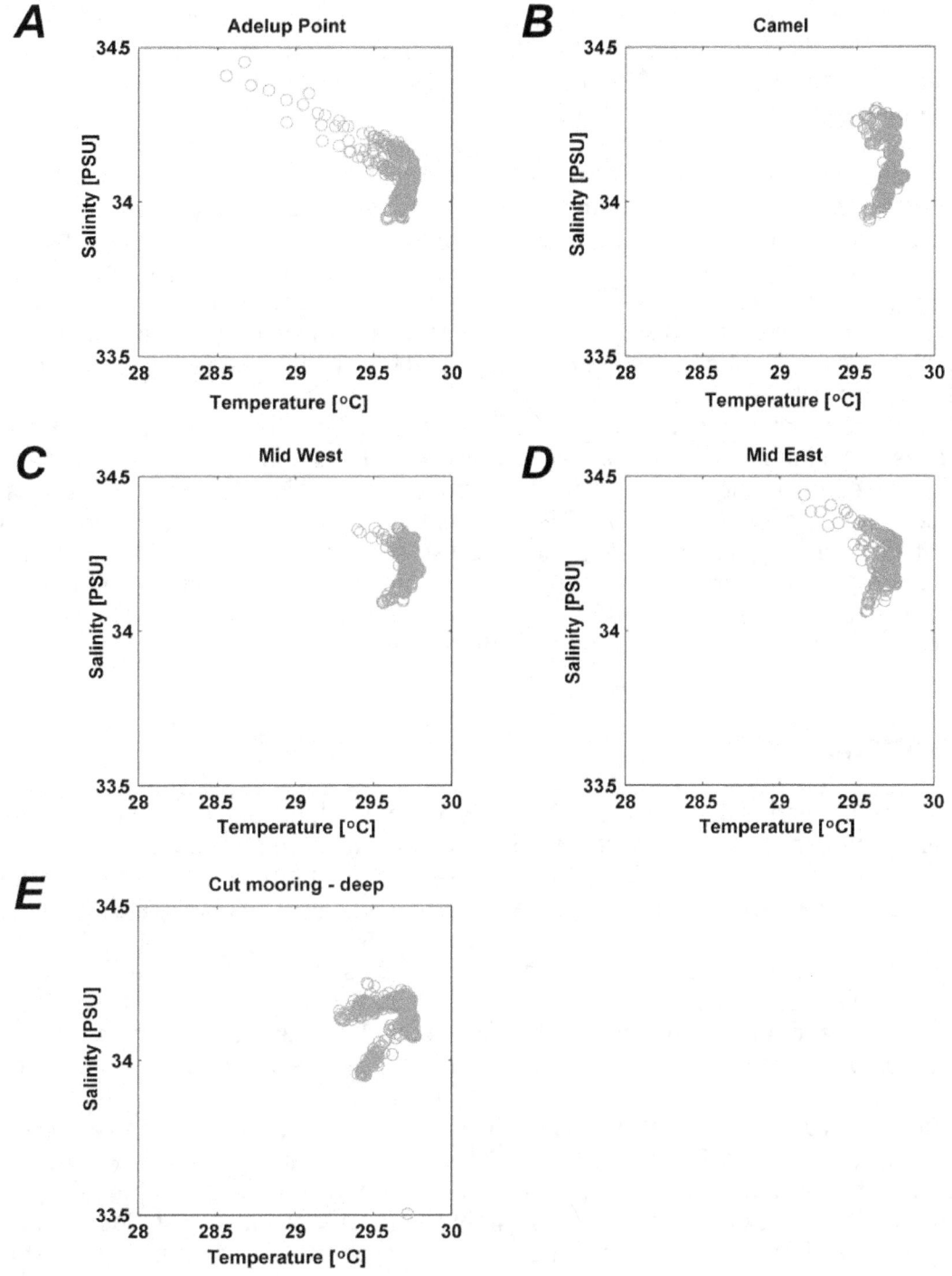

Figure 34. Variation in salinity, in Practical Salinity Units, and temperature, in degrees Celsius, at the deep sites during the bar break and flood. *A,* Adelup Point. *B,* Camel Rock. *C,* Mid West. *D,* Mid East. *E,* Cut Mooring-deep. All of the deep sites show a small decrease in salinity during the flood but not as great a decrease as the sensors close to the surface, suggesting that the freshwater plume was confined relatively close to the surface.

that immediately preceded the drop in temperature and reversals in current direction (west and offshore). The strong oscillating vertical component of velocity (currents rapidly alternating between upward and downward flow) is typically an indication of higher-frequency internal waves following the head of the internal tidal bore (Storlazzi and others, 2003). Tidal currents were generally small, less than 0.1 m/s, while internal motions associated with internal tides generated currents greater than 0.2 m/s.

The relationships between temperature and salinity for the deep and shallow sites during internal tides as compared to the other forcing conditions are shown in figs. 37 and 38, respectively. The temperature and salinity during internal tides at the shallow sites (blue) show very little change from the tide, wind, and wave forcing conditions (red). The deep sites show the internal tides have significantly different temperature-salinity relationships (fig. 38). At all of the deep sites, the relationship between temperature-salinity during internal tides lies between the trends during wave events (cooler for a given salinity) and those during tide and wind conditions (warmer for a given salinity). The internal tide signal has the highest salinities and lowest temperatures of all of the forcing conditions.

The occurrence of the internal tides appears to show a seasonal trend. The large decreases in temperature and increases in salinity occurred primarily during the wet season and were not observed during the more consistent trade wind forcing of the dry season (fig. 7). The water temperatures measured by the CTs deployed in WAPA during the dry season were substantially cooler than those measured in the wet season. The resulting lower thermal stratification during the dry season on the fore reef may be insufficient to support internal motions, similar to the relationships observed elsewhere between thermal stratification and the presence of internal motions (Storlazzi and others, 2003).

## Conclusions

In all, more than 6 million measurements of meteorologic and oceanographic forcing and the resulting water column properties were made along west-central Guam and in War-in-the-Pacific National Historical Park (WAPA) during the 6-month period between July 2007 and January 2008. Key findings from these measurements and analyses include the following.

1) Circulation in the bay was primarily to the west and offshore due to the sea floor morphology in the Cut and the trade winds blowing in an east-to-west direction. The current speeds are greater off Camel Rock and Adelup Point than in the Cut, except at the surface during strong wind and/or large wave conditions, when there is very strong near-surface offshore flow out of the Cut.

2) Overall, turbidity was relatively low in the bay and was similar to levels measured elsewhere along west-central Guam. Due to biofouling of the optical sensors, long, continuous records and variations in turbidity at the shallow and deep sites were not obtained. Additional high-frequency, long-duration turbidity data to compare to established water quality thresholds would provide more complete information to NPS and other agencies tasked with maintaining water quality.

3) The delivery of sediment to Asan Bay during this experiment was primarily from erosion of the carbonate reef flat sediment and terrestrial sediment discharged from the Asan River. A buildup of sand at the mouth of Asan River reduced the amount of surface freshwater and sediment that entered the bay. During times of high precipitation and/or large wave events, the bar was breached, discharging terrestrial sediment and freshwater directly into the bay. The terrestrial sediment plume observed during the period of study was relatively confined to the surface and

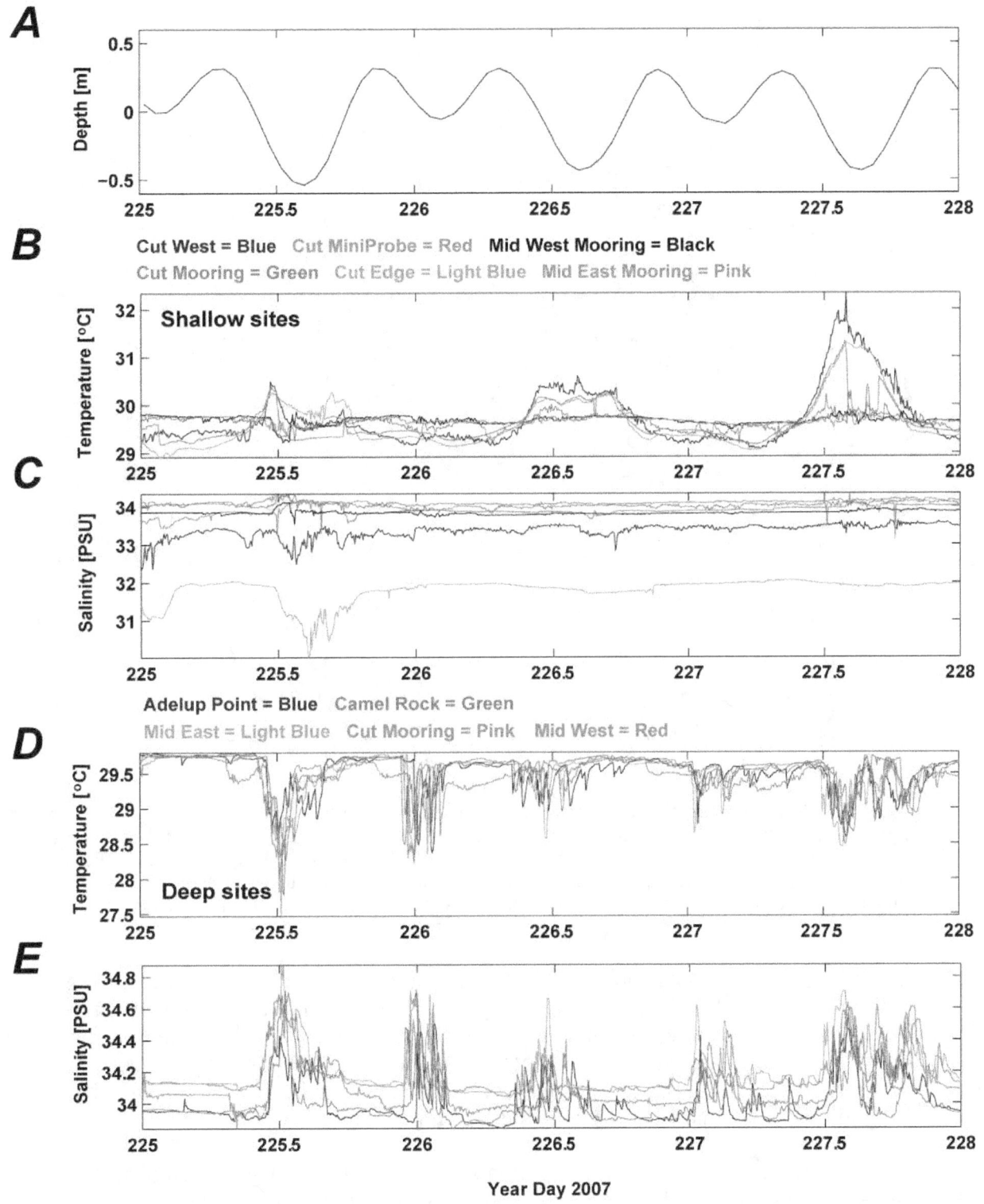

Figure 35. Tide, temperature, and salinity data from the deep and shallow sites during a period of internal tides. *A,* Tide, in meters. *B,* Temperature at the shallow sites, in degrees Celsius. *C,* Salinity at the shallow sites, in Practical Salinity Units. *D,* Temperature at the deep sites, in degrees Celsius. *E,* Salinity at the deep sites, in Practical Salinity Units. The shallow sites show increases in temperature due to daily heating and very little variation in salinity during this time period. The deep sites show a significant decrease in temperature and increase in salinity with the falling tide indicating internal motions moving deep oceanic water up onto the shelf.

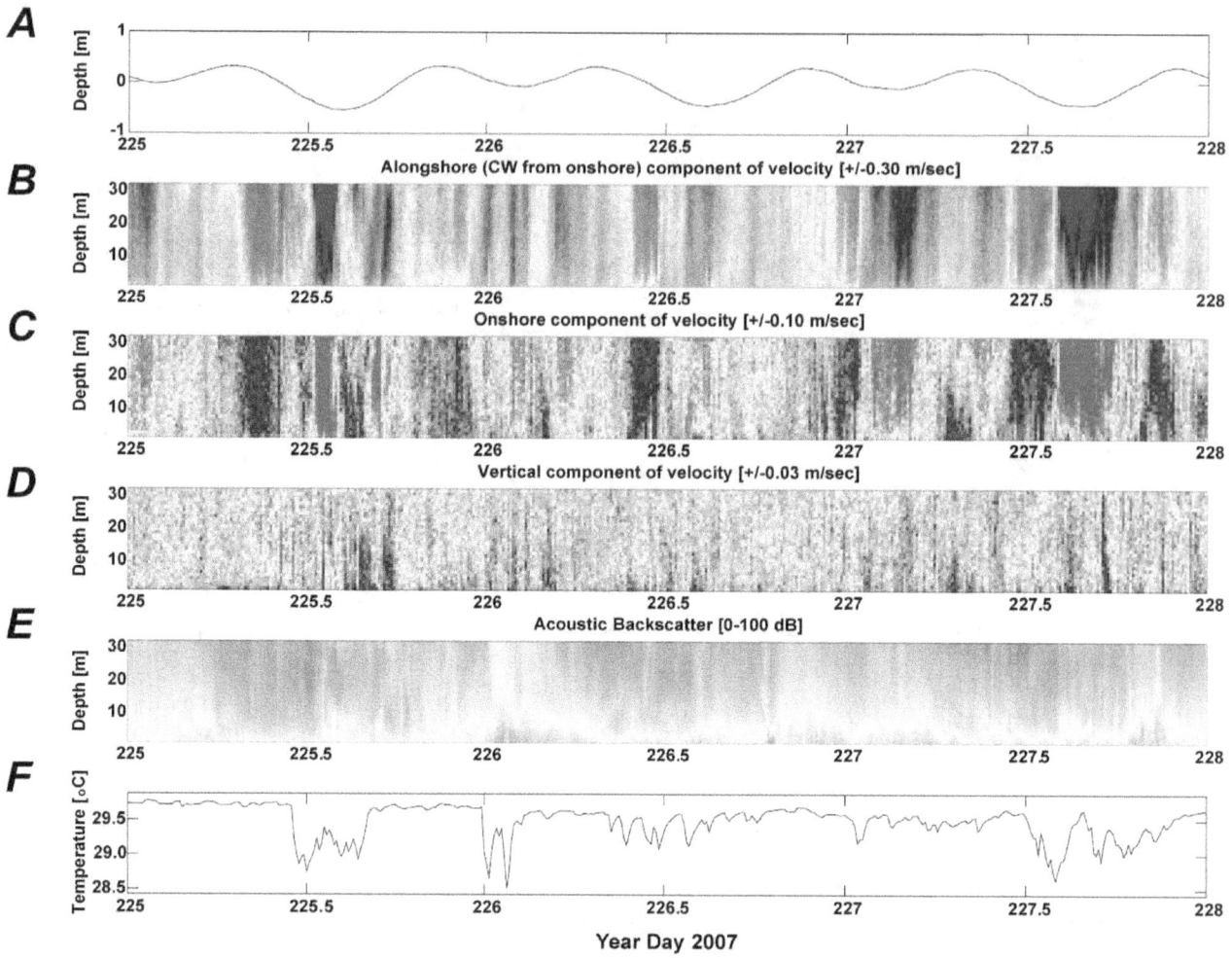

Figure 36. Tide, current, and temperature data during a period of internal tides. *A,* Tide, in meters. *B,* Alongshore current velocity, in meters per second. *C,* Onshore current velocity, in meters per second. *D,* Vertical current velocity, in meters per second. *D,* Acoustic backscatter, in decibels. *E,* Temperature, in degrees Celsius. The various components of velocity show strong stratification during the internal tidal bores, resulting in large drops in temperature and increased acoustic backscatter, suggesting the advection of either sediment or biologic material by the bores. The internal tides appear to occur during the ebbing tide at the deep sites.

was not as large as during previous floods (D. Minton, written communication). The largest flux of terrestrial sediment and freshwater was transported offshore through the Cut. Very little freshwater and terrestrial sediment made its way to the eastern and western sides of the bay. Additional *in situ* water samples collected during a large flood for suspended sediment data to compare to established water quality thresholds would provide more complete information to NPS and other agencies tasked with maintaining water quality.

4) While the sea floor sediment was primarily calcareous gravelly sand, the material collected in sediment traps was predominantly terrigenous sandy mud. The fact that a substantial (40-85 percent) portion of the sediment collected in the traps was fine-grained terrestrial particles, which are likely under-represented in the traps due to their slow settling velocities relative to the currents speeds and wave-orbital velocities, suggests that significant volumes of terrigenous sediment are advected through this area. These particles can block sunlight and thus reduce PAR and photosynthesis, and/or desorb nutrients or contaminants. The absence of these particles on

Blue = Internal Tide    Red = All other conditions

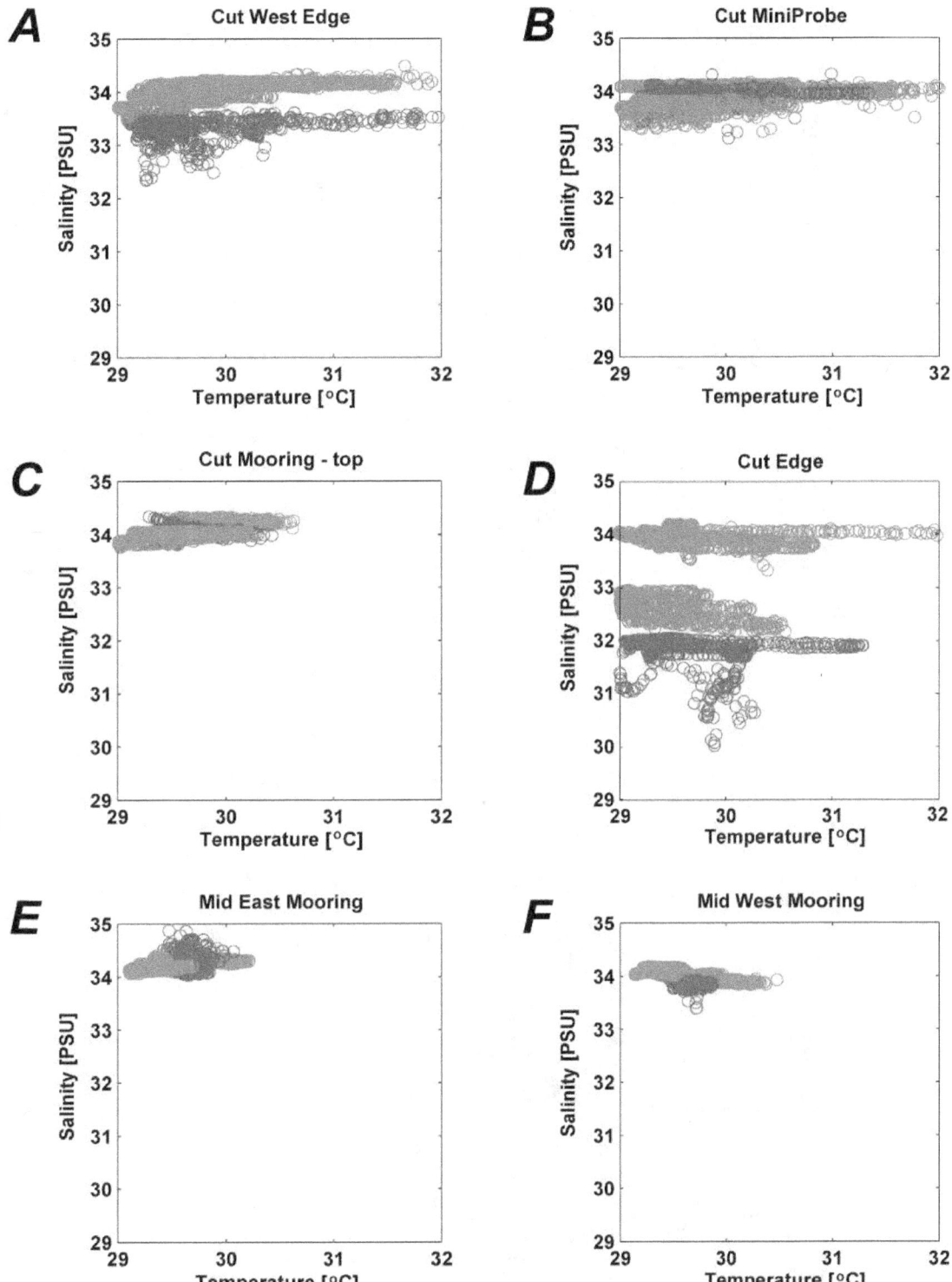

Figure 37. Variation in salinity, in Practical Salinity Units, and temperature, in degrees Celsius, at the shallow sites during a period of internal tides. *A,* Cut West Edge. *B,* Cut MiniProbe. *C,* Cut Mooring-top. *D,* Cut Edge. *E,* Mid East Mooring; *F,* Mid West Mooring. The temperature and salinity during internal tidal bores follow the same pattern as the other conditions at the shallow sites.

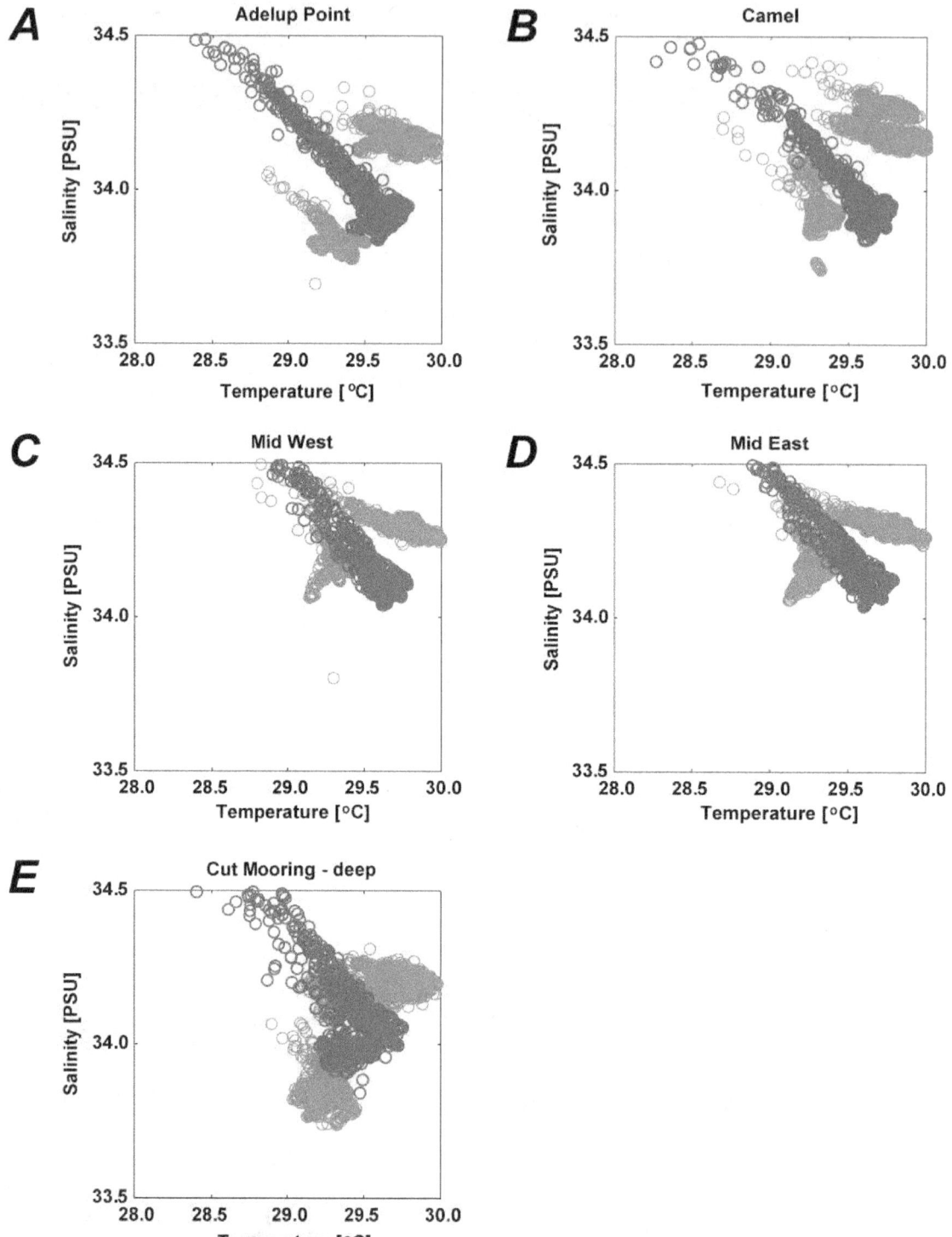

Figure 38. Variation in salinity, in Practical Salinity Units, and temperature, in degrees Celsius, at the deep sites during a period of internal tides. *A,* Adelup Point. *B,* Camel Rock. *C,* Mid West. *D,* Mid East. *E,* Cut Mooring–deep. The temperature and salinity during internal tidal bores show a strong trend of increasing salinity with decreasing temperature, indicative of deep water being pumped up onto the insular shelf that has a distinct temperature-salinity relationship from the other forcing conditions.

the sea floor, however, shows that these particles do not reside on the sea floor for long durations under the wave and current conditions in the bay during the period of study. A large input of sediment followed by low-energy conditions, however, could result in significant temporary deposition of terrestrial material in the bay. In the Cut, the trap collection rates approached 70 mg/cm$^2$/day, potentially resulting in mortality of adult corals (Phillips and Fabricius, 2003); the trap collection rates measured elsewhere in Asan Bay were substantially below levels thought to negatively impact corals, suggesting that if the corals are responding to terrestrial sediment, it may be due to associated nutrients or contaminants that adhere to the sediment. In order to determine if nutrients or contaminants are associated with the terrestrial sediment, the Park could work with an environmental toxicologist to test the terrestrial sediment collected in sediment traps, resident fish, and/or crustaceans for nutrients and contaminants to compare to established water and sediment quality thresholds.

5) Internal tidal bores appear to be an important mechanism for the delivery of deep oceanic water onto the insular shelf as measured by the temperature and salinity sensors at the deep (20 m) sites. The drop in temperature and increase in salinity was observed frequently during falling tides; these signals were indistinguishable during trade-wind conditions when the temperature and salinity signals were highly variable. The pumping of deep, oceanic water into deep areas has potentially both beneficial and detrimental implications. These internal tides can advect cooler, deep, nutrient-rich waters into the oligotrophic surface waters, potentially benefiting corals by offsetting thermally-induced coral stress and providing nutrients. Conversely, these bores could also advect nutrient- and contaminant-laced material from deep-water sewage outfalls or from submarine groundwater discharging terrestrial wastewater injection well material. In order to determine the potential range of influence of these bores, the Park could deploy a number of temperature and salinity sensors in a cross-shore transect of moorings to determine from what depth these bores can transport material up into the Park's coral reef ecosystem.

These data provide information on the nature and controls on flow and water column properties along west-central Guam during nontyphoon conditions. A number of interesting phenomena were observed that indicate the complexity of coastal circulation and sediment dynamics in Asan Bay and may help to better understand the implications of the processes on coral reef health.

# Acknowledgments

This work was carried out as part of the USGS's Coral Reef Project as part of an effort in the U.S. and its trust territories to better understand the affect of geologic processes on coral reef systems. Dwayne Minton (former NPS-WAPA Natural Resource Division chief scientist, now at the U.S. Fish and Wildlife Service) and Sarah Creachbaum (NPS-WAPA superintendent) overextended themselves to establish this cooperative study. The Allison Palmer, Holley Voegtle, and Mark Capone of the NPS-WAPA Natural Resource Division contributed substantially to this project in innumerous ways, and without their efforts none of this would have been possible. Todd Genereux expertly captained the *F/V Heavy Metal* while Edwin Elias (USGS) provided insight and advice in performing the numerical circulation modeling. Mike Torresan and Angela Lam processed the sediment samples described in this report. The NPS maintenance and office staff graciously donated their time, effort, and space during our numerous field operations. The Pacific Cooperative Studies Unit provided some of the instruments used in this field experiment. Dave Burdick and Victor Torres (Guam Bureau of Statistics and Plans) provided the vertical aerial imagery and lidar data used throughout this report. Dan Hoover (USGS) and Kurt Rosenberger (USGS) contributed numerous excellent suggestions and a timely review of our work.

## References Cited

Baker, E.T., Milburn, H.B., and Tennant D.A., 1988, Field assessment of sediment trap efficiency under varying flow conditions: Journal of Marine Research, v. 46, p. 573-592.

Barber, S.G., 2002, Laboratory procedures and grain size analysis of terrigenous and carbonaceous sediment of the fringing reef of Molokai, Hawaii: California, San Francisco State University, thesis, p. 4-13, appendix A.

Booij, N., Ris, R.C., and Holthuijsen, L.H., 1999. A third-generation wave model for coastal regions, Part I- Model description and validation: Journal of Geophysical Research, v. 104, p. 7649-7666.

Bothner, M.H., Reynolds, R.L., Casso, M.A., Storlazzi, C.D., and Field, M.E., 2006, Quantity, composition, and source of sediment collected in sediment traps along the fringing coral reef off Molokai, Hawaii: Marine Pollution Bulletin, v. 52, p. 1034–1047.

Coastal and Hydraulics Laboratory, U.S. Army Corps of Engineers, 2008, Wave Information Studies (WIS) hindcast wave climate information for U.S. coastal waters; Stations #134 and #142, available online at http://frf.usace.army.mil/cgi-bin/wis/pac/pac_main.html, last accessed July 2009.

Center for Operational Oceanographic Products and Services, National Oceanographic and Atmospheric Administration, 2008, Historic tide data for Apra Harbor, Guam, CO-OPS ID: 1630000, available online at http://tidesandcurrents.noaa.gov/

Deines, K.L., 1999, Backscatter estimation using broadband acoustic Doppler current profilers: RD Instruments Application Note FSA-008, 5 p.

Delft3D User Manual, 2006, Delft3D-FLOW User Manual- Simulation of multi-dimensional hydrodynamic flows and transport phenomena, including sediment: the Netherlands, Delft Hydraulics.

Forestry and Soil Resources Division, Guam Department of Agriculture, 1999, Five year plan: Department of Agriculture.

Gardner, W.D., Richardson, M.J., Hinga, K.R. and Biscaye, P.E., 1983, Resuspension measured with sediment traps in a high-energy environment: Earth and Planetary Science Letters, v. 66, p. 262-278.

Holthuijsen, L.H., Booij, N., and Ris, R.C., 1993, A spectral wave model for the coastal zone: New Orleans, 2nd International Symposium on Ocean Wave Measurement and Analysis, p. 630-641.

Lander, M.A., and Guard, C.P., 2003, Creation of a 50-year rainfall database, annual rainfall climatology, and annual rainfall distribution map for Guam: University of Guam Water and Environmental Research Institute, Technical Report No. 102, 32 p.

Leendertse, J.J., 1987, A 3-dimensional alternating direction implicit model with iterative Fourth order dissipative non-linear advection terms: Rijkswaterstaat, Report WD-3333-NETH,.

Lesser, G.L., 2000, Computation of 3-dimensional suspended sediment transport within the Delft3D-FLOW module, Report WL | Delft Hydraulics Z2396, Delft, 123 p.

Marszalek, D.S., 1981, Impact of dredging on a subtropical reef community- Southeastern Florida, U.S.A: Proceedings of the 4th International Coral Reef Congress, p. 147-153.

Minton, D., 2005, Fire, erosion, and sedimentation in the Asan-Piti Watershed and War in the Pacific NHP, Guam: Report prepared for the National Park Service, 99 p.

Minton, D., Lundgren, I., and Pakenham, A., 2007. A two-year study of coral recruitment and sedimentation in Asan Bay, Guam: Final report prepared for the National Park Service, 41 p.

National Centers for Coastal Ocean Science, National Oceanographic and Atmospheric Administration, 2005, Shallow-water benthic habitats of American Samoa, Guam, and the Commonwealth of the Northern Mariana Islands: NOAA Technical Memorandum NOS NCCOS 8, Biogeography Branch, available online at http://ccma.nos.noaa.gov/products/biogeography/U.S._pac_terr/htm/data.htm, last accessed July 2009.

National Climate Data Center, National Oceanographic and Atmospheric Administration, 2008, Andersen Air Force Base Guam hourly surface weather data, GSOD ID: 912180, available online at http://cdo.ncdc.noaa.gov/CDO/cdo, last accessed July 2009.

National Park Service, 2007, War-in-the-Pacific National Historical Park, available online at http://www.nps.gov/wapa/, last accessed July 2009.

National Resource Conservation Service, 1996, Ugam Watershed Management Plan, Territory of Guam. Agana, Guam: U.S. Department of Agriculture, Pacific Basin Area.

Office of Insular Affairs, Department of the Interior, 2008, Guam overview, available online at http://www.doi.gov/oia/Islandpages/gumpage.htm, last accessed July 2009.

Pacific Islands Global Climate Observing System, Guam Climate Office, 2008, The weather and climate of Guam, available online at http://pi-gcos.org/guam/default.htm, last accessed July 2009.

Phillip, E., and Fabricius, K.E., 2003, Photophysiological stress in scleractinian corals in response to short-term sedimentation: Journal of Experimental Marine Biology and Ecology, v. 287, p. 57-78.

Porter, V., Leberer, T., Gawel, M., Gutierrez, J., Burdick, D., Torres, V., and Lujan, E., 2005, The State of Coral Reef Ecosystems of Guam, in J. Waddell, ed., The state of coral reef ecosystems of the United States and Pacific Freely Associated State: 2005: Silver Spring, NOAA Technical

Memorandum NOS NCCOS 11. NOAA/NCCOS Center for Coastal Monitoring and Assessment Biogeography Team, Maryland, 533 p.

Richmond, R. and Hunter, C., 1990, Reproduction and recruitment of corals- Comparisons among the Caribbean, tropical Pacific and the Red Sea: Marine Ecology Progress Series, v. 60, p. 185-202.

Ris, R.C., Booij, N., and Holthuijsen, L.H., 1999, A third-generation wave model for coastal regions, Part II- verification: Journal of Geophysical Research, v. 104, no. 4, p. 7649-7666.

Stelling, G.S., 1984, On the construction of computational methods for shallow water flow problems: Rijkswaterstaat, The Hague, communication series no. 35.

Storlazzi, C.D., McManus, M.A., and Figurski, J.D., 2003, Long-term high-frequency ADCP and temperature measurements along central California- Insights into upwelling and internal waves on the inner shelf: Continental Shelf Research, v. 23, p. 901-918.

Walstra, D.J., Roelvink, J.A., and Groeneweg, J., 2000, Calculation of wave-driven currents in a 3D mean flow model: Proceedings of 27th Conference on Coastal Engineering, p. 1050-1063.

# Additional Digital Information

For additional information on the instrument deployments, please see:
http://walrus.wr.usgs.gov/infobank/b/b107wp/html/b-1-07-wp.meta.html
http://walrus.wr.usgs.gov/infobank/b/b207wp/html/b-2-07-wp.meta.html
http://walrus.wr.usgs.gov/infobank/b/b108wp/html/b-1-08-wp.meta.html

For an online PDF version of this report, please see:
http://pubs.usgs.gov/of/2009/1195/

For more information on the U.S. Geological Survey Western Region's Coastal and Marine Geology Team, please see:
http://walrus.wr.usgs.gov/

For more information on the U.S. Geological Survey's Coral Reef Project, please see:
http://coralreefs.wr.usgs.gov/

# Direct Contact Information

General Project Information
Michael E. Field (USGS Coral Reef Project Chief):          mfield@usgs.gov

Regarding this Report:
Curt D. Storlazzi (Chief Scientist):          cstorlazzi@usgs.gov

## Table 1. Experiment personnel.

| Person | Affiliation | Responsibilities |
|---|---|---|
| Curt Storlazzi | USGS | Chief scientist, diver |
| Kathy Presto | USGS | Oceanographer, instrument specialist |
| Joshua Logan | USGS | Information specialist, diver |
| Greg Piniak | NOAA | Diver |
| Dave Gonzales | USGS | Instrument specialist |
| Tom Reiss | USGS | Dive safety officer |
| Allison Palmer | NPS | Biologic Resource Division specialist, diver |
| Holley Voegtle | NPS | Biologic Resource Division specialist, diver |
| Mark Capone | NPS | Biologic Resource Division chief, diver |
| Todd Genereux | F/V Heavy Metal | Vessel captain |

## Table 2. Instrument package sensors.

| Site Name | Depth [m] | Sensors |
|---|---|---|
| Two Lover's Point | 10 | NIWA Dobie-A wave/tide gauge |
| | 10 | Seabird SBE-37SI Microcat conductivity-temperature sensor |
| Adelup Point | 20 | RD Instruments 600 kHz Workhorse Monitor acoustic Doppler current profiler |
| | 20 | Aquatec/Seapoint 200-TY optical backscatter sensor |
| | 20 | Seabird SBE-37SI Microcat conductivity-temperature sensor |
| | 20 | Onset HOBO UA-002-08 pendant light and temperature logger |
| | 19 | Sediment tube trap |
| Mid East | 20 | RD Instruments 600 kHz Workhorse Monitor acoustic Doppler current profiler |
| | 20 | Aquatec/Seapoint 200-TY optical backscatter sensor |
| | 20 | Seabird SBE-37SI Microcat conductivity-temperature sensor |
| | 20 | Onset HOBO UA-002-08 pendant light and temperature logger |
| | 19 | Sediment tube trap |
| Mid East mooring | 3 | Aquatec/Seapoint 200-TYT optical backscatter sensor with temperature sensor |
| | 3 | Seabird SBE-37SI Microcat conductivity-temperature sensor |
| Cut mooring | 20 | Seabird SBE-37SI Microcat conductivity-temperature sensor |
| | 19 | Sediment tube trap |
| | 3 | Aquatec/Seapoint 200-TYT optical backscatter sensor with temperature sensor |
| | 3 | Seabird SBE-37SI Microcat conductivity-temperature sensor |
| Cut MiniProbe | 10 | Nortek 2 MHz Aquadopp acoustic Doppler current profiler |
| | 10 | Seabird SBE-37SI Microcat conductivity-temperature sensor |
| | 10 | Onset HOBO UA-002-08 pendant light and temperature logger |
| | 9 | Sediment tube trap |
| Cut edge | 1 | YSI 6600 EDS Sonde conductivity-temperature-turbidity sensor |
| Cut West edge | 1 | Aquatec/Seapoint 200-TYT optical backscatter sensor with temperature sensor |
| | 1 | Seabird SBE-37SI Microcat conductivity-temperature sensor |
| Mid West | 20 | RD Instruments 600 kHz Workhorse Monitor acoustic Doppler current profiler |
| | 20 | Aquatec/Seapoint 200-TY optical backscatter sensor |
| | 20 | Seabird SBE-37SI Microcat conductivity-temperature sensor |
| | 20 | Onset HOBO UA-002-08 pendant light and temperature logger |
| | 19 | Sediment tube trap |
| Mid West mooring | 3 | Aquatec/Seapoint 200-TYT optical backscatter sensor with temperature sensor |
| | 3 | Seabird SBE-37SI Microcat conductivity-temperature sensor |
| Camel Rock | 20 | RD Instruments 600 kHz Workhorse Monitor acoustic Doppler current profiler |
| | 20 | Aquatec/Seapoint 200-TY optical backscatter sensor |
| | 20 | Seabird SBE-37SI Microcat conductivity-temperature sensor |
| | 20 | Onset HOBO UA-002-08 pendant light and temperature logger |
| | 19 | Sediment tube trap |
| Agat Point | 10 | NIWA Dobie-A wave/tide gauge |
| | 10 | Seabird SBE-37SI Microcat conductivity-temperature sensor |
| Weather Station | - | NovaLynx WS-16N-A weather station |
| River Gauge | - | Onset HOBO U20-01-Ti pressure logger |
| Terrestrial Camera System | - | USGS Terrestrial Imaging System |

**Table 3.** Instrument package location information.

| Site name | Latitude [decimal degrees] | Longitude [decimal degrees] |
|---|---|---|
| Two Lover's Point | 13.53620 | 144.80119 |
| Adelup Point | 13.48320 | 144.72878 |
| Mid East | 13.48064 | 144.71797 |
| Cut mooring | 13.47638 | 144.71547 |
| Cut MiniProbe | 13.47432 | 144.71594 |
| Cut West | 13.47501 | 144.71487 |
| Mid West | 13.47788 | 144.71265 |
| Camel Rock | 13.48175 | 144.70439 |
| Agat Point | 13.37939 | 144.64516 |
| Weather Station | 13.47471 | 144.71857 |
| River Gauge | 13.47269 | 144.71337 |
| Terrestrial Camera System | 13.46002 | 144.71517 |

**Table 4.** Water column profiler cast location and depth information.

| Cast Number/site | Location | Latitude [decimal degrees] | Longitude [decimal degrees] | Depth [m] |
|---|---|---|---|---|
| 1 | Two Lovers Point | 13.536 | 144.800 | 30 |
| 2 | Tumon Bay | 13.514 | 144.797 | 21 |
| 3 | Ypao Point | 13.508 | 144.775 | 16 |
| 4 | Hagatna Bay | 13.488 | 144.764 | 11 |
| 5 | Hagatna Boat Basin | 13.485 | 144.748 | 15 |
| 6 | Adelup Point | 13.483 | 144.729 | 21 |
| 7 | Asan Bay East | 13.480 | 144.719 | 21 |
| 8 | Asan Cut | 13.475 | 144.716 | 19 |
| 9 | Asan Cut Mooring | 13.476 | 144.715 | 13 |
| 10 | Asan Cut Offshore 1 | 13.478 | 144.715 | 33 |
| 11 | Asan Cut Offshore 2 | 13.482 | 144.714 | 120 |
| 12 | Asan Bay West | 13.478 | 144.713 | 17 |
| 13 | Camel Rock | 13.481 | 144.705 | 18 |
| 14 | Piti | 13.472 | 144.692 | 12 |
| 15 | Luminao Reef East | 13.467 | 144.664 | 29 |
| 16 | Luminao Reef West | 13.469 | 144.640 | 12 |
| 17 | Apra Harbor Western Shoal | 13.453 | 144.654 | 13 |
| 18 | Apra Outer Harbor 2 | 13.451 | 144.644 | 37 |
| 19 | Apra Outer Harbor 1 | 13.451 | 144.633 | 51 |
| 20 | Apra Harbor Entrance | 13.453 | 144.621 | 28 |
| 21 | Orote Point | 13.445 | 144.618 | 26 |
| 22 | Blue Hole | 13.436 | 144.626 | 35 |
| 23 | Apuntua Point | 13.421 | 144.639 | 18 |
| 24 | Neye Island North | 13.416 | 144.645 | 11 |
| 25 | Apaca Beach | 13.410 | 144.653 | 13 |
| 26 | Apaca Point North | 13.405 | 144.657 | 17 |
| 27 | Apaca Point South | 13.400 | 144.652 | 28 |
| 28 | Agat North | 13.389 | 144.650 | 16 |
| 29 | Alutom Island | 13.382 | 144.645 | 16 |
| 30 | Agat Boat Basin Entrance | 13.368 | 144.643 | 10 |
| 31 | Anae Island | 13.358 | 144.636 | 17 |

## Table 5. Sediment sample location and depth information.

| USGS sample identifier | Location | Sample type | NPS location identifier | Average trap collection rate [mg/cm$^2$/day] | Latitude [decimal degrees] | Longitude [decimal degrees] | Depth [m] |
|---|---|---|---|---|---|---|---|
| GU-0108-001 | Mid West | Sea floor | K-60 | - | 13.47793 | 144.71257 | 20 |
| GU-0108-002 | Cut mooring | Sea floor | O-60 | - | 13.47638 | 144.71548 | 20 |
| GU-0108-003 | Mid East | Sea floor | Q-60 | - | 13.48064 | 144.71798 | 20 |
| GU-0108-004 | Camel Rock | Sediment trap | - | 5.55 | 13.46002 | 144.71518 | 19 |
| GU-0108-005 | Mid West | Sediment trap | K-60 | 4.77 | 13.47793 | 144.71257 | 19 |
| GU-0108-006 | Cut mooring | Sediment trap | O-60 | 46.52 | 13.47638 | 144.71548 | 19 |
| GU-0108-007 | Cut MiniProbe | Sediment trap | - | 60.34 | 13.47433 | 144.71594 | 9 |
| GU-0108-008 | Mid East | Sediment trap | Q-60 | 5.29 | 13.48064 | 144.71798 | 19 |
| GU-0108-009 | Adelup Point | Sediment trap | - | 6.30 | 13.48320 | 144.72878 | 19 |

## Table 6. Meteorological statistics.

All values were calculated for 2007 Year Days 208-390; wind direction is "Going to".

| Site name | Mean ± 1 std. deviation | Minimum | Maximum |
|---|---|---|---|
| Sea level barometric pressure [mB] | 1,007.9±1.6 | 1,001 | 1,012.69 |
| Air temperature [°C] | 27.71±2.12 | 22.94 | 36.5 |
| Precipitation [mm] | 0.13±0.81 | 0 | 25.25 |
| Wind speed [m/s] | 1.53±0.87 | 0 | 8.25 |
| Wind direction [°] | 311.4±61.5 | 180.19 | 179.62 |

## Table 7. Current statistics.

Current direction is "Going To.

| Site name | Parameter | Depth [m] | Mean ± 1 std. deviation | Minimum | Maximum |
|---|---|---|---|---|---|
| Adelup Point | Speed [m/s] | 2 | 0.10±0.06 | 0.00 | 0.42 |
| | Direction [°] | 2 | 174.5±77.4 | 2.3 | 358.4 |
| | Speed [m/s] | 18 | 0.04±0.03 | 0.00 | 0.16 |
| | Direction [°] | 18 | 160.2±105.4 | 0.0 | 359.7 |
| Mid East* | Speed [m/s] | 2 | 0.18±0.11 | 0.00 | 0.70 |
| | Direction [°] | 2 | 235.7±46.5 | 0.3 | 359.6 |
| | Speed [m/s] | 18 | 0.05±0.04 | 0.00 | 0.23 |
| | Direction [°] | 18 | 142.0±101.3 | 0.2 | 359.7 |
| Cut MiniProbe | Speed [m/s] | 1 | 0.26±0.18 | 0.00 | 1.07 |
| | Direction [°] | 1 | 282.5±79.0 | 0.02 | 360 |
| | Speed [m/s] | 9 | 0.16±0.14 | 0.00 | 0.91 |
| | Direction [°] | 9 | 155.2±130.5 | 0 | 360 |
| Mid West | Speed [m/s] | 2 | 0.08±0.05 | 0.01 | 0.32 |
| | Direction [°] | 2 | 201.7±68.0 | 0.7 | 359.0 |
| | Speed [m/s] | 18 | 0.04±0.03 | 0.00 | 0.23 |
| | Direction [°] | 18 | 195.3±111.3 | 0.0 | 359.7 |
| Camel Rock | Speed [m/s] | 2 | 0.17±0.11 | 0.00 | 0.75 |
| | Direction [°] | 2 | 205.0±81.2 | 0.0 | 359.4 |
| | Speed [m/s] | 18 | 0.11±0.08 | 0.00 | 0.53 |
| | Direction [°] | 18 | 201.3±92.0 | 0.0 | 359.2 |

*Values were calculated for days 2007 Year Days 309.5-390, otherwise values were calculated for 2007 Year Days 208-390.

# Table 8. Wave statistics.

Wave direction is "Going To.

| Site name | Parameter | Mean ± 1 std. deviation | Minimum | Maximum |
|---|---|---|---|---|
| Two Lover's Point* | Height [m] | 0.37±0.33 | 0.05 | 2.14 |
| | Period [s] | 8.4±1.6 | 4.2 | 13.9 |
| Adelup Point | Height [m] | 0.68±0.30 | 0.23 | 2.00 |
| | Period [s] | 6.4±1.5 | 3.0 | 11.2 |
| | Direction [°] | 86.8±137.7 | 0.0 | 360.0 |
| Mid East | Height [m] | 0.69±0.29 | 0.25 | 2.26 |
| | Period [s] | 5.2±1.1 | 3.0 | 9.6 |
| | Direction [°] | 105.0±106.9 | 1.0 | 360.0 |
| Cut MiniProbe | Height [m] | 0.12±0.06 | 0.03 | 0.50 |
| | Period [s] | 8.9±1.3 | 5.7 | 16.6 |
| | Direction [°] | 148.9±28.3 | 0.3 | 352.7 |
| Mid West | Height [m] | 0.65±0.26 | 0.27 | 1.77 |
| | Period [s] | 5.4±1.2 | 3.2 | 10.7 |
| | Direction [°] | 39.7±340.1 | 0 | 360.0 |
| Camel Rock | Height [m] | 0.85±0.35 | 0.3 | 2.31 |
| | Period [s] | 6.2±1.4 | 3.3 | 11.1 |
| | Direction [°] | 348.1±159.4 | 0.0 | 360.0 |
| Agat Point* | Height [m] | 0.35±0.31 | 0.04 | 1.90 |
| | Period [s] | 7.9±1.6 | 4.5 | 12.9 |

*Values were calculated for days 2007 Year Days 208-300, otherwise values were calculated for 2007 Year Days 208-390.

## Table 9: Temperature statistics.

All statistics are from YD 208-300.

| Site name | Depth [m] | Mean ± 1 std. deviation [°C] | Minimum [°C] | Maximum [°C] |
|-----------|-----------|------------------------------|--------------|--------------|
| Two Lover's Point | 10 | 29.61±0.19 | 27.91 | 30.14 |
| Adelup Point | 20 | 29.57±0.23 | 27.09 | 30.08 |
| Mid East | 20 | 29.57±0.24 | 27.20 | 30.12 |
| Mid East mooring | 3 | 29.66±0.20 | 29.02 | 30.61 |
| Cut mooring | 20 | 29.50±0.24 | 27.39 | 30.06 |
| Cut mooring | 3 | 29.65±0.28 | 28.88 | 31.09 |
| Cut MiniProbe | 10 | 29.54±0.57 | 27.79 | 32.64 |
| Cut edge | 1 | 29..55±0.92 | 27.03 | 34.21 |
| Cut West edge | 1 | 29.65±0.51 | 28.18 | 32.35 |
| Mid West | 20 | 29.58±0.23 | 27.30 | 30.20 |
| Mid West mooring | 3 | 29.67±0.21 | 29.02 | 30.88 |
| Camel Rock | 20 | 29.61±0.21 | 27.27 | 30.20 |
| Agat Point | 10 | 29.71±0.23 | 28.59 | 30.70 |

## Table 10. Salinity statistics.

All statistics are from YD 208-300.

| Site name | Depth [m] | Mean ± 1 std. deviation [PSU] | Minimum [PSU] | Maximum [PSU] |
|-----------|-----------|-------------------------------|---------------|---------------|
| Two Lover's Point [1] | 10 | 34.12±0.17 | 30.80 | 34.75 |
| Adelup Point [2] | 20 | 33.96±0.24 | 32.84 | 34.81 |
| Mid East [3] | 20 | 34.22±0.12 | 33.81 | 34.88 |
| Mid East mooring [3] | 3 | 34.16±0.15 | 32.80 | 34.50 |
| Cut mooring [4] | 20 | 33.93±0.33 | 32.11 | 34.44 |
| Cut mooring [4] | 3 | 34.03±0.21 | 32.11 | 34.45 |
| Cut MiniProbe [5] | 10 | 33.74±0.35 | 29.19 | 34.48 |
| Cut edge [5] | 1 | 30.14±0.95 | 21.71 | 32.30 |
| Cut West edge [6] | 1 | 33.67±0.40 | 28.03 | 34.49 |
| Mid West [7] | 20 | 34.23±0.11 | 33.39 | 34.83 |
| Mid West mooring [7] | 3 | 34.01±0.18 | 30.77 | 34.49 |
| Camel Rock [8] | 20 | 33.97±0.18 | 32.82 | 34.71 |
| Agat Point [9] | 10 | 34.10±0.20 | 32.93 | 34.46 |

## Table 11. Turbidity statistics from the SLOBSs.

Biofouling occurred during much of this period, so statistics are only from 2007 Year Days 208-225

| Site name | Depth [m] | Mean ± 1 std. deviation [NTU] | Minimum [NTU] | Maximum [NTU] |
|---|---|---|---|---|
| Adelup Point | 20 | 1.89±0.69 | 0.83 | 4.80 |
| Mid East | 20 | 2.33±1.20 | 1.44 | 15.13 |
| Mid East mooring | 3 | 12.34±6.43 | 0.06 | 161.41 |
| Cut mooring | 3 | 11.46±7.26 | 0.45 | 88.12 |
| Cut edge | 1 | 10.14±9.38 | 5.04 | 144.51 |
| Cut West edge | 1 | 9.24±44.35 | 0 | 1,180.30 |
| Mid West | 20 | 4.14±1.20 | 2.31 | 6.06 |
| Mid West mooring | 3 | 1.93±0.66 | 0 | 6.46 |
| Camel Rock | 20 | 1.21±0.62 | 0.61 | 4.87 |

## Table 12. Turbidity statistics calculated from the ADCPs.

Statistics are from 2007 Year Days 208-390.

| Site name | Depth [m] | Mean ± 1 std. deviation [NTU] | Minimum [NTU] | Maximum [NTU] |
|---|---|---|---|---|
| Adelup Point | 20 | 1.83±0.14 | 1.42 | 2.45 |
| Mid East | 20 | 3.96±0.54 | 2.37 | 6.67 |
| Cut MiniProbe | 9 | 28.25±5.00 | 18.55 | 44.83 |
| Mid West | 20 | 4.25±0.62 | 2.83 | 7.38 |
| Camel Rock | 20 | 1.03±0.30 | 0.08 | 2.94 |

## Table 13. Light statistics.

These data are from 2007 Year Days 309- 350 when concurrent, reliable data were recorded.
Mean difference = mean [(surface observation from Weather Station) – (sea floor observation at instrument package)]

| Site name | Depth [m] | Mean ± 1 std. deviation [mE] | Mean Difference [mE] | Mean Difference [percent] | Maximum [mE] |
|---|---|---|---|---|---|
| Weather Station | - | 29,864±51,056 | - | - | 231,470 |
| Cut Mooring | 20 | 417±1,067 | 29,447 | 1.4 | 9,645 |
| Mid East | 20 | 1,253±2,227 | 28,642 | 4.2 | 13,778 |
| Cut MiniProbe | 10 | 830±1,617 | 28,619 | 2.7 | 11,288 |
| Mid West | 20 | 1,245±2,312 | 29,034 | 4.2 | 14,702 |

Table 14. Sediment sample grain size information.

| USGS sample identifier | Gravel [percent] | Sand [percent] | Silt [percent] | Clay [percent] | Mean size [mm] |
|---|---|---|---|---|---|
| GU-0108-001 | 18.29 | 77.87 | 1.77 | 2.07 | 0.4232 |
| GU-0108-002 | 13.87 | 82.60 | 1.59 | 1.94 | 0.4359 |
| GU-0108-003 | 18.79 | 76.52 | 2.89 | 1.81 | 0.3721 |
| GU-0108-004 | 2.54 | 37.65 | 47.61 | 12.20 | 0.0338 |
| GU-0108-005 | 1.22 | 31.28 | 51.92 | 15.59 | 0.0242 |
| GU-0108-006 | 0.00 | 58.27 | 31.46 | 10.26 | 0.0463 |
| GU-0108-007 | 0.79 | 71.39 | 21.23 | 6.59 | 0.0812 |
| GU-0108-008 | 6.36 | 25.67 | 51.32 | 16.65 | 0.0280 |
| GU-0108-009 | 0.74 | 34.11 | 53.93 | 11.21 | 0.0299 |

# Table 15. Sediment sample composition information.

| USGS sample identifier | Component analyzed | Total inorganic carbon [percent] | Calcium carbonate [percent] | Terrigenous [percent] |
|---|---|---|---|---|
| GU-0108-001 | Bulk | 11.20 | 93.27 | 6.73 |
| GU-0108-002 | Bulk | 9.88 | 82.34 | 17.66 |
| GU-0108-003 | Bulk | 10.60 | 88.26 | 11.74 |
| GU-0108-004 | Bulk | 1.86 | 15.52 | 84.48 |
| GU-0108-005 | Bulk | 4.25 | 35.39 | 64.61 |
| GU-0108-006 | Bulk | 7.00 | 58.27 | 41.73 |
| GU-0108-007 | Bulk | 7.24 | 60.30 | 39.70 |
| GU-0108-008 | Bulk | 4.10 | 34.17 | 65.83 |
| GU-0108-009 | Bulk | 2.03 | 16.90 | 83.10 |
| | | | | |
| GU-0108-001 | Sand | 11.40 | 94.94 | 5.06 |
| GU-0108-002 | Sand | 10.52 | 87.65 | 12.35 |
| GU-0108-003 | Sand | 11.12 | 92.66 | 7.34 |
| GU-0108-004 | Sand | 11.22 | 93.43 | 6.57 |
| GU-0108-005 | Sand | 9.96 | 82.93 | 17.07 |
| GU-0108-006 | Sand | 7.97 | 66.38 | 33.62 |
| GU-0108-007 | Sand | 7.72 | 64.32 | 35.68 |
| GU-0108-008 | Sand | 10.35 | 86.22 | 13.78 |
| GU-0108-009 | Sand | 10.97 | 91.42 | 8.58 |
| | | | | |
| GU-0108-001 | Silt | 10.29 | 85.69 | 14.31 |
| GU-0108-002 | Silt | 5.35 | 44.53 | 55.47 |
| GU-0108-003 | Silt | 9.23 | 76.92 | 23.08 |
| GU-0108-004 | Silt | 10.64 | 88.64 | 11.36 |
| GU-0108-005 | Silt | 9.69 | 80.74 | 19.26 |
| GU-0108-006 | Silt | 7.73 | 64.41 | 35.59 |
| GU-0108-007 | Silt | 7.27 | 60.54 | 39.46 |
| GU-0108-008 | Silt | 9.68 | 80.64 | 19.36 |
| GU-0108-009 | Silt | 10.81 | 90.07 | 9.93 |
| | | | | |
| GU-0108-001 | Clay | 8.26 | 68.84 | 31.16 |
| GU-0108-002 | Clay | 4.20 | 34.95 | 65.05 |
| GU-0108-003 | Clay | 6.55 | 54.60 | 45.40 |
| GU-0108-004 | Clay | 7.41 | 61.70 | 38.30 |
| GU-0108-005 | Clay | 6.17 | 51.36 | 48.64 |
| GU-0108-006 | Clay | 4.56 | 37.97 | 62.03 |
| GU-0108-007 | Clay | 4.56 | 37.96 | 62.04 |
| GU-0108-008 | Clay | 6.52 | 54.33 | 45.67 |
| GU-0108-009 | Clay | 7.91 | 65.91 | 34.09 |

**Table 16.** Delft3D model settings.

| Module | Parameter | Value | Description |
|--------|-----------|-------|-------------|
| Flow | Grid cells | 135,137 | number of cells: East-west and North-south, respectively |
| Flow | Lat | +13.5 | latitude for Coriolis forcing (decimal degrees North) |
| Flow | thick | 5, 8, 14, 23, 23, 14, 8, 5 | thickness of the sigma layers (%) |
| Flow | $\Delta t$ | 6 | flow time step (s) |
| Flow | $\rho_w$ | 1023 | water density (kg/m2) |
| Flow | K | 1 | horizontal eddy viscosity |
| Flow | N | 1 | horizontal eddy diffusitivity |
| Flow | V | 9.9e-005 | Vertical eddy diffusitivity |
| Flow | C | 65 | Chézy coefficient |
| Flow | Dryflc | 0.1 | threshold depth |
| Flow | Rouwav | Fredsoe 1984 | stress formulation due to wave forces |
| Flow | Tkemod | K-epsilon | turbulence closure formulation |
| Flow | Cstbnd | true | boundary condition |
| Flow | Bndast | true | astronomic water Levels boundary condition constituents: K1, M2, S2, O1, N2, Q2 |
| Flow | Slipcon | free | wall roughness scheme |
| Flow | Advect | cyclic | advection scheme for momentum |
| | | | |
| Wave | Grid cells | 137,132 | number of cells: East-west and North-south, respectively |
| Wave | Dir space | circle | directional space |
| Wave | $\Delta\theta$ | 10 | spectral resolution (degrees) |
| Wave | freq min | 0.05 | lowest discrete frequency (Hz) |
| Wave | freq high | 1.00 | highest discrete frequency (Hz) |
| Wave | freq bins | 24 | number of frequency bins |
| Wave | Shape | JONSWAP; 3.3 | spectral shape; peak enhancement factor |
| Wave | Tp | peak | wave period definition |
| Wave | Dirspread | cosine power | directional spreading definition |
| Wave | dp min | 0.05 | threshold depth (m) |
| Wave | setup | false | wave-related water level setup |
| Wave | convention | nautical | orientation |
| Wave | forcing | wave energy dissipation rate | computation of wave forces |
| Wave | generation mode | 3-rd | generation mode for physics |
| Wave | wave breaking | B&J model | depth-induced breaking model |
| Wave | alfa1 | 1 | coefficient for wave energy dissipation in the B&J model |
| Wave | gamma2 | 0.73 | breaker parameter in the B&J model |
| Wave | triads (LTA) | false | non-linear triad wave-wave interactions |
| Wave | bottom friction | JONSWAP; 0.067 | bottom friction formulation; coefficient for bottom friction |
| Wave | diffraction | false | diffraction |
| Wave | wind growth | true | formulation for exp1ntial wave growth |
| Wave | white capping | true | formulation for white capping |
| Wave | quadruplets | true | quadruplet wave-wave interactions |
| Wave | ref | activated | refraction is activated for waves propagation in spectral space |
| Wave | freq | true | frequency shift activated for wave propagation spectral space |
| Wave | CDD | 0.5 | diffusion of implicit scheme in directional space |
| Wave | CSS | 0.5 | diffusion of implicit scheme in frequency space |
| Wave | accuracy | 98 | accuracy criteria iterative computation (%) |
| Wave | max iterations | 20 | maximum number of iterations |
| Wave | Hs | 0.02 | fraction relative change with respect to mean value Hs |
| Wave | Tm01 | 0.02 | fraction relative change respect to mean mean value Tm01 |
| | | | |
| MORSYS | CompMode | stationary | computational mode |
| MORSYS | CompInt | 60 | coupling interval of wave module and flow module (min) |

**Table 17.** Delft3D model run information.

| Run ID | Time frame (h) | Wave height (m) | Wave period (s) | Wave direction (°) | Wave directional spread (°) | Wind speed (m/s) | Wind direction (°) |
|--------|---------------|-----------------|-----------------|--------------------|-----------------------------|------------------|--------------------|
| w08 | 24 | 1.5 | 8 | 45 | 4 | 5 | 45 |
| w09 | 24 | 0.5 | 5 | 45 | 4 | 5 | 45 |
| w10 | 24 | 1.5 | 8 | 315 | 4 | 5 | 45 |
| w11 | 24 | 0.5 | 5 | 315 | 4 | 5 | 45 |

# Appendix 1

## ADCP information

RD Instruments 600 kHz Workhorse Monitor upward-looking acoustic Doppler current profiler
s/n: 2074, 2432, 7747, and 7749

| | |
|---|---|
| Transmitting Frequency: | 614 kHz |
| Depth of Transducer: | 20 m |
| Blanking Distance: | 0.25 m |
| Height of First Bin above Bed: | 1.11 m |
| Bin Size: | 0.5 m |
| Number of Bins: | 48 |
| Operating Mode: | High-resolution, broad bandwidth |
| Sampling Frequency: | 2 Hz |
| Time per Ping: | 00:03.00 |
| Pings per Ensemble: | 100 |
| Profile Ensemble Interval: | 0:10:00.00 |
| Wave Ensemble Interval: | 2:00:00.00 |
| Sound Speed Calculation: | Set salinity, updating temperature via sensor |

Nortek Instruments 2 MHz Aquadopp upward-looking acoustic Doppler current profiler
s/n: 1862

| | |
|---|---|
| Depth of Transducer: | 10m |
| Blanking Distance: | 0.25 m |
| Height of First Bin above Bed: | 0.75m |
| Bin Size: | 0.50m |
| Number of Bins: | 20 |
| Average interval: | 0:02:00.00 |
| Profile interval: | 0:10:00.00 |
| Wave interval: | 1:00:00.00 |
| Wave cell size: | 2 m |
| Operating Mode: | High-resolution |
| Sound Speed Calculation: | Set salinity, updating temperature via sensor |

Data Processing:

The RDI current data were processed using the WinADCP program and the wave data using the WavesMon program. The Nortek current data were processed using the Prof2NDP program and the wave data were processed using the QuickWave program.

The data were averaged over 1 hour ensembles, all of the spurious data above the water surface were removed and all of the data in bins where the beam correlation dropped below 80% were removed for visualization and analysis.

# Appendix 2

WTG, CT, SLOBS, LS, and PL sensor information

NIWA Dobie-A wave and tide gauges (WTG)
        s/n: 2000-18 and 2000-21
| | |
|---|---|
| Depth of Transducer: | 10 m |
| Operating Mode: | Water level time series |
| Sampling Frequency: | 2 Hz |
| Measurements per Burst: | 512 |
| Time Between Bursts: | 01:00:00.00 |

Seabird Microcat SBE-37SM temperature-conductivity (CT) sensors
        s/n: 3372, 3800, 3801, 3825, 3830, 3833, 4088, 4089, 4360, 4368, 4369, and 4421
| | |
|---|---|
| Sampling Frequency: | 2 Hz |
| Measurements per Burst: | 8 |
| Time Between Bursts: | 00:05:00.00 |

Aquatec/Seapoint 200-TY self-logging optical backscatter sensors (SLOBS)
        s/n: 371-013, 371-026
Aquatec/Seapoint 210-TYT self-logging optical backscatter sensors (SLOBS)
        s/n: 024-002, 024-005, 024-006, 024-007, 024-012 and 024-013
| | |
|---|---|
| Sampling Frequency: | 2 Hz |
| Measurements per Burst: | 30 |
| Time Between Bursts: | 00:05:00.00 |

Onset HOBO UA-002-08 pendant light and temperature logger (LS)
        s/n: 998614, 998691, 998623, 1019880, 1019865, and 1176239
| | |
|---|---|
| Sampling Frequency: | 2 Hz |
| Measurements per Burst: | 30 |
| Time Between Bursts: | 01:00:00.00 |

Onset HOBO U20-01-Ti pressure logger (PL)
        s/n: 1115706 and 1115707
| | |
|---|---|
| Sampling Frequency: | 2 Hz |
| Measurements per Burst: | 30 |
| Time Between Bursts: | 01:00:00.00 |

Data Processing:
The WTG data were processed using the PEDP program and the CT data were processed using the SBEDataProcessing program.

The WTG 2 Hz water level data were averaged over the entire 20 min burst to compute tidal height, while hourly significant wave height and dominant wave period data were computed from the 2 Hz data using spectral methods. The CT and SLOBS data were post-processed for visualization and analysis by removing all instantaneous (only 1 data point in time) data spikes that exceeded the deployment mean + 3 standard deviations.

# Appendix 3

WS and TIS information

NovaLynx WS-16N-A Marine-grade Weather Station Comp1nts:
| | |
|---|---|
| Anemometer: | 200-05106-MA (marine model) |
| Temperature & Relative Humidity: | 110-WS-16TH-A w/radiation shield |
| Barometric Pressure Sensor: | 110-WS-16BP |
| Rain Gauge: | 110-WS-16RC |

| | |
|---|---|
| Sampling Frequency: | 1 Hz |
| Measurements per Burst: | 1800 |
| Time Between Bursts: | 00:30:00.00 |

USGS Terrestrial Imaging System Components:
| | |
|---|---|
| Camera: | Nikon CoolPix 8700 8-megapixel digital camera |
| Programmable Automated Controller: | Campbell Scientific Scientific CR200 |
| Sampling Frequency: | Every 2 hours from 06:00 to 18:00 ChST |


# Appendix 4

Water column profiler and sensor information

Instruments:
| | |
|---|---|
| Seabird 19plus CTD sensor; s/n: | 4299 |
| D&A Instruments OBS-3 sensor; s/n: | 19830-2000 |
| Licor #II-193SA PAR sensor; s/n: | SPQA-3562 |
| Seabird SBE 43 oxygen sensor; s/n: | 430731 |
| Wet Labs 9502016 fluorometer; s/n: | WS3-017  0-75 ug/l |
| Sampling Frequency: | 4 Hz |

Position Information:
Garmin GPS-76 GPS; s/n: 80207465; USGS/CRP unit#1

Data Processing:
The profiler data were processed using the SBEDataProcessing program.

The data were averaged into 0.5 m vertical bins and all of the spurious data marked by a flag in the raw data were removed for visualization and analysis. Stratification were measured as the difference between the mean of the top 3 bins (0.5-1.5 m below the surface) and the bottom 3 bins (0.5-1.5 m above the bed).

# Appendix 5

## Water column profiler log: July 2007

| Cast Number/site | Date | Time [ChST] | Latitude [decimal degrees] | Longitude [decimal degrees] | Depth [m] |
|---|---|---|---|---|---|
| 1 | 07/23/2007 | 0822 | 13.53672 | 144.80059 | 29 |
| 2 | 07/23/2007 | 0832 | 13.51426 | 144.79677 | 23 |
| 3 | 07/23/2007 | 0840 | 13.50742 | 144.77473 | 16 |
| 4 | 07/23/2007 | 0848 | 13.48848 | 144.76447 | 11 |
| 5 | 07/23/2007 | 0855 | 13.48479 | 144.74831 | 14 |
| 6 | 07/23/2007 | 0903 | 13.48320 | 144.72878 | 20 |
| 7 | 07/23/2007 | 0910 | 13.48057 | 144.71804 | 14 |
| 8 | 07/23/2007 | 0916 | 13.47622 | 144.71546 | 15 |
| 9 | 07/23/2007 | 0920 | 13.47512 | 144.71552 | 9 |
| 10 | 07/23/2007 | 0927 | 13.47853 | 144.71523 | 30 |
| 11 | 07/23/2007 | 0932 | 13.48161 | 144.71469 | 61 |
| 12 | 07/23/2007 | 0937 | 13.47795 | 144.71273 | 26 |
| 13 | 07/23/2007 | 0944 | 13.48171 | 144.70415 | 12 |
| 14 | 07/23/2007 | 0951 | 13.47211 | 144.69160 | 13 |
| 15 | 07/23/2007 | 1002 | 13.46706 | 144.66369 | 12 |
| 16 | 07/23/2007 | 1010 | 13.46951 | 144.63997 | 12 |
| 17 | 07/23/2007 | 1019 | 13.45320 | 144.62177 | 20 |
| 18 | 07/23/2007 | 1026 | 13.44509 | 144.61854 | 21 |
| 19 | 07/23/2007 | 1034 | 13.43629 | 144.62650 | 67 |
| 20 | 07/23/2007 | 1044 | 13.42078 | 144.63941 | 19 |
| 21 | 07/23/2007 | 1201 | 13.41633 | 144.64517 | 10 |
| 22 | 07/23/2007 | 1207 | 13.41017 | 144.65266 | 10 |
| 23 | 07/23/2007 | 1213 | 13.40507 | 144.65708 | 16 |
| 24 | 07/23/2007 | 1219 | 13.40071 | 144.65190 | 13 |
| 25 | 07/23/2007 | 1226 | 13.38908 | 144.64973 | 18 |
| 26 | 07/23/2007 | 1232 | 13.38146 | 144.64550 | 12 |
| 27 | 07/23/2007 | 1244 | 13.35779 | 144.63586 | 12 |
| 28 | 07/23/2007 | 1250 | 13.36796 | 144.64242 | 9 |

# Appendix 6

## Water column profiler log: November 2007

| Cast Number/site | Date | Time [ChST] | Latitude [decimal degrees] | Longitude [decimal degrees] | Depth [m] |
|---|---|---|---|---|---|
| 1 | 11/04/2007 | 0806 | 13.53661 | 144.80054 | 29 |
| 2 | 11/04/2007 | 0817 | 13.51443 | 144.79661 | 23 |
| 3 | 11/04/2007 | 0825 | 13.50746 | 144.77473 | 16 |
| 4 | 11/04/2007 | 0833 | 13.48852 | 144.76447 | 11 |
| 5 | 11/04/2007 | 0838 | 13.48478 | 144.74823 | 14 |
| 6 | 11/04/2007 | 0844 | 13.48331 | 144.72869 | 20 |
| 7 | 11/04/2007 | 0849 | 13.48049 | 144.71814 | 14 |
| 8 | 11/04/2007 | 0854 | 13.47507 | 144.71553 | 15 |
| 9 | 11/04/2007 | 0856 | 13.47622 | 144.71539 | 9 |
| 10 | 11/04/2007 | 0858 | 13.47861 | 144.71524 | 30 |
| 11 | 11/04/2007 | 0901 | 13.48178 | 144.71468 | 61 |
| 12 | 11/04/2007 | 0907 | 13.47798 | 144.71271 | 26 |
| 13 | 11/04/2007 | 0911 | 13.48156 | 144.70463 | 12 |
| 14 | 11/04/2007 | 0917 | 13.47210 | 144.69168 | 13 |
| 15 | 11/04/2007 | 0925 | 13.46706 | 144.66370 | 12 |
| 16 | 11/04/2007 | 0931 | 13.46959 | 144.63996 | 12 |
| 17 | 11/04/2007 | 0938 | 13.45312 | 144.62176 | 20 |
| 18 | 11/04/2007 | 0943 | 13.44528 | 144.61842 | 21 |
| 19 | 11/04/2007 | 0949 | 13.43609 | 144.62640 | 67 |
| 20 | 11/04/2007 | 1102 | 13.42089 | 144.63927 | 19 |
| 21 | 11/04/2007 | 1116 | 13.41631 | 144.64515 | 10 |
| 22 | 11/04/2007 | 1120 | 13.41022 | 144.65272 | 10 |
| 23 | 11/04/2007 | 1124 | 13.40514 | 144.65710 | 16 |
| 24 | 11/04/2007 | 1128 | 13.40074 | 144.65189 | 13 |
| 25 | 11/04/2007 | 1132 | 13.38907 | 144.64969 | 18 |
| 26 | 11/04/2007 | 1136 | 13.38156 | 144.64542 | 12 |
| 27 | 11/04/2007 | 1143 | 13.35789 | 144.63587 | 12 |
| 28 | 11/04/2007 | 1148 | 13.36792 | 144.64244 | 9 |

# Appendix 7

## Water column profiler log: February 2008

| Cast Number/site | Date | Time [ChST] | Latitude [decimal degrees] | Longitude [decimal degrees] | Depth [m] |
|---|---|---|---|---|---|
| 1 | 02/01/2008 | 0927 | 13.53635 | 144.80042 | 27 |
| 2 | 02/01/2008 | 0935 | 13.51442 | 144.79658 | 20 |
| 3 | 02/01/2008 | 0943 | 13.50750 | 144.77483 | 16 |
| 4 | 02/01/2008 | 0952 | 13.48834 | 144.76444 | 11 |
| 5 | 02/01/2008 | 0958 | 13.48473 | 144.74823 | 14 |
| 6 | 02/01/2008 | 1004 | 13.48314 | 144.72869 | 20 |
| 7 | 02/01/2008 | 1011 | 13.48032 | 144.71871 | 9 |
| 8 | 02/01/2008 | 1016 | 13.47496 | 144.71561 | 12 |
| 9 | 02/01/2008 | 1020 | 13.47607 | 144.71524 | 9 |
| 10 | 02/01/2008 | 1023 | 13.47838 | 144.71502 | 30 |
| 11 | 02/01/2008 | 1028 | 13.48174 | 144.71448 | 76 |
| 12 | 02/01/2008 | 1034 | 13.47782 | 144.71266 | 15 |
| 13 | 02/01/2008 | 1039 | 13.48147 | 144.70477 | 15 |
| 14 | 02/01/2008 | 1047 | 13.47190 | 144.69170 | 11 |
| 15 | 02/01/2008 | 1056 | 13.46704 | 144.66390 | 27 |
| 16 | 02/01/2008 | 1105 | 13.46935 | 144.63995 | 11 |
| 17 | 02/01/2008 | 1121 | 13.45258 | 144.65411 | 12 |
| 18 | 02/01/2008 | 1126 | 13.45125 | 144.64443 | 35 |
| 19 | 02/01/2008 | 1131 | 13.45139 | 144.63309 | 47 |
| 20 | 02/01/2008 | 1138 | 13.45286 | 144.62148 | 26 |
| 21 | 02/01/2008 | 1145 | 13.44533 | 144.61823 | 24 |
| 22 | 02/01/2008 | 1151 | 13.43615 | 144.62632 | 32 |
| 23 | 02/01/2008 | 1158 | 13.42065 | 144.63927 | 17 |
| 24 | 02/01/2008 | 1203 | 13.41617 | 144.64490 | 10 |
| 25 | 02/01/2008 | 1208 | 13.41022 | 144.65251 | 12 |
| 26 | 02/01/2008 | 1212 | 13.40525 | 144.65710 | 15 |
| 27 | 02/01/2008 | 1216 | 13.40038 | 144.65181 | 26 |
| 28 | 02/01/2008 | 1224 | 13.38909 | 144.64968 | 15 |
| 29 | 02/01/2008 | 1229 | 13.38166 | 144.64507 | 15 |
| 30 | 02/01/2008 | 1234 | 13.36789 | 144.64251 | 9 |
| 31 | 02/01/2008 | 1238 | 13.35794 | 144.63583 | 14 |